MasterChef

THE CLASSICS

WITH A TWIST

MasterChef

THE CLASSICS

WITH A TWIST

CONTENTS

SIDE DISHES

DESSERTS AND BAKING

JOHN TORODE

While judging *MasterChef* over the years, Gregg and I have met more talented chefs than I can count. This book contains the cream of the crop: eleven MasterChef champions from the last ten years who wowed us on the programme and have since gone on to even better and greater things in the world of food.

To be a MasterChef champion takes more than simply knowing how to cook well. The difference between a good plate of food and an extraordinary dish, between a chef and a MasterChef, is character. Every winner can instinctively take an ordinary recipe and put something of themselves in it, and in the process produce something unique. That might involve drawing upon the flavours of their childhood, swapping in an entirely unexpected ingredient, or plating a dish a certain way. Both on the show and afterwards, our MasterChefs have proven they can do this. They know what it takes to put personality in their food.

But, as you read the recipes in this book, remember: every MasterChef starts out as an amateur. They didn't train for years at a culinary school. They are ordinary women and men with a passion for food and a determination to live up to that passion. They have the confidence to try new ideas, and are patient enough to try again – and again and again – if those ideas don't quite work the first time around. If you have that same passion, then congratulations: you are on your way to becoming a MasterChef.

Whether you dream of being on the show or simply want to put a twist on a favourite dish, take inspiration from the recipes in this book. Each one has been transformed by one of our MasterChefs from a familiar classic to something extraordinary. Try them for yourself to see how the champions have experimented with presentation ideas and flavour combinations. Once you're ready, have a go yourself. Reinvent your favourite recipe, deconstruct a classic dessert, and dare to inject a little personality into your food. Who knows? One day we might have the honour of judging your food on the show.

GREGG WALLACE

There's a lot of talk on *MasterChef* about "taking a dish to the next level", as if a plate of food could take a ride in an elevator. Really, it's all about being brave enough to try new ideas. If a contestant sees an opportunity to do something different, to push their food just that bit further, they should take it. It might work, it might not. But, if it works, chances are they'll end up in our good books.

Next-level cooking doesn't need to mean using expensive or unpronounceable ingredients. It doesn't have to mean adding 27 different drizzles and smears and foams for the sake of it, either. A good dish can easily be ruined with too much fussing about. Sometimes all you need to make a fantastically delicious meal is a handful of simple, good-quality ingredients, chosen well and cooked well.

Many of the recipes in this collection do exactly that. They take known and loved classic dishes and reimagine them, daring to try out something a little less familiar if it means taking those classics to new heights. These brand-new recipes might surprise you with the combination of ingredients, or the way they are presented, but they are not beyond the reach of the average home cook. These are everyday recipes, but not quite as you know them. In other words, they have been taken to the next level.

Are there drizzles and jellies and the like in this book as well? Absolutely. This is a *MasterChef* book, after all. But, whenever a recipe involves a little bit of fuss, you'll notice that those added details don't distract you from the main dish. They are there to enhance the main component, not outshine it. It's all about balance, in terms of both flavour and presentation.

This book contains 100 examples of how you can put a twist on a classic, along with plenty of advice from the MasterChefs, who know exactly what it takes to produce next-level cooking. If you want to do the same, you'll do well to follow their example, and to try out their dishes so you can see how it's done.

Gregg

STARTERS

PEA AND WHITE TRUFFLE SOUP WITH PARMESAN GALETTES

My favourite way of serving this is to use elegant coffee cups and saucers. The Parmesan galettes need to be wide enough to balance safely on top of each serving cup.

250g (9oz) frozen peas or petit pois, plus 1 tsp for the galettes

450ml (15fl oz) hot vegetable stock

a few thyme sprigs, leaves picked

salt and freshly ground black pepper

1–2 tbsp crème fraîche (optional)

white truffle oil, to serve

FOR THE GALETTES

80g (3oz) Parmesan cheese, finely grated

2 slices Serrano ham

1 packet pea shoots

Small handful of mint tips (the very tiny new growth buds at the end of the stem) or 6 mint leaves

viola flowers

1 Put the peas in a bowl, then pour over boiling water and leave to stand for about 5 minutes. Drain.

2 Put the peas (setting aside 1 tsp for the galettes), stock, and thyme leaves in a blender and blend until smooth and combined, in batches if necessary. Add more stock if the soup is too thick. Season well with salt and pepper, and blend again.

3 Make the Parmesan galettes. Heat a heavy-based non-stick frying pan over a medium heat and sprinkle 4 thin layers of Parmesan to make a galette wide enough for your serving cups. When the cheese starts to melt, wait about 2 minutes, until it turns golden and bubbly. Immediately remove from the heat, leave for about 1 minute, then transfer to a wire rack.

4 Finely shred the ham into strips. Scatter each galette with the reserved petit pois, viola petals, pea shoots, and mint.

5 To serve, stir the crème fraîche (if using) into the soup, use a hand-held blender to froth up the liquid, pour into serving bowls or cups, and spoon a head of froth over each. Add a few drops of truffle oil to each cup and top with a Parmesan galette balanced on each cup.

MAKE IT *extraordinary*

White truffle oil brings a distinctive aromatic flavour to classic pea soup.

Crisp, savoury Parmesan galettes are topped by a fresh, colourful garnish.

PREP 15 MINUTES
COOK 3 MINUTES
SERVES 4-6

BUTTERNUT SQUASH HARIRA

This warming Moroccan version of a butternut squash soup takes on a rich flavour from a blend of spices, and is thickened with the addition of lentils. Serve harira with a sprinkling of crushed cumin seeds and a generous squeeze of lemon juice.

Fry off the spices to release their aroma into the harira base.

2 tbsp olive oil

2 onions, finely chopped

3 garlic cloves, finely chopped

salt

1 cinnamon stick

1 tsp ground ginger

2 tbsp ground coriander

2 tbsp ground cumin

1 large butternut squash or 2 small ones, halved, peeled, deseeded, and chopped into bite-sized chunks

75g (2½oz) red lentils

1.4 litres (2½ pints) hot vegetable stock

2 tbsp flour

TO SERVE

crushed cumin seeds

olive oil, to drizzle

a small handful of coriander leaves

1-2 lemons, cut into wedges

1 Heat the oil in a large pan, add the onions and garlic, and cook over a low heat for 6-8 minutes, or until the onions are soft and translucent. Season with salt, then add the spices and cook until fragrant. Once the pan is dry, add the butternut squash and lentils, and fry for another minute. Add the stock.

2 Simmer the soup for 15-20 minutes, until the lentils are tender. Remove the cinammon stick.

3 Mix together the flour and 100ml (3½fl oz) cold water, stirring until it becomes a smooth paste. Stir the flour mixture into the soup, and continue to cook until it has been cooked out, for about 10 minutes. Season with salt to taste.

4 To serve, drizzle over some olive oil and garnish with crushed cumin seeds, coriander leaves, and a lemon wedge.

PREP 10 MINUTES
COOK 1 HOUR
SERVES 8

LEEK AND POTATO SOUP WITH LEEK OIL AND POTATO NESTS

A topping of crispy potato nests gives this classic, creamy starter a satisfying crunch, while a drizzle of bright green leek oil intensifies the flavours.

200ml (7fl oz) groundnut oil

3 large leeks, trimmed and finely sliced, trimmings reserved

2 tbsp vegetable oil

25g (scant 1oz) butter

1 large onion, finely sliced

2 celery sticks, finely sliced

5 sprigs of thyme

2 bay leaves

600g (1lb 5oz) potatoes, peeled and cut into 2.5cm (1in) cubes

1.2 litres (2 pints) chicken or vegetable stock

150ml (5fl oz) double cream

salt and freshly ground black pepper

2 tbsp finely sliced chives

FOR THE POTATO NESTS

2 litres (3½ pints) oil, for deep-fat frying

1 large potato, peeled, and spiralized into spaghetti-like strands

1 First, make the leek oil. Heat the groundnut oil to 160°C (325°F), add the leek trimmings, and leave to cool. When cool, blitz in a food processor and then pass through muslin and leave to drain for 1 hour. Squeeze out the excess, discard the leek trimmings, and set aside the oil until ready to serve.

2 Make the potato nests. Preheat a deep-fat fryer to 180°C (350°F). Twist a handful of spiralized potato into a nest shape and place into a pea ladle. Lower the ladle into the fryer and fry the nest on the ladle for about 1 minute, until crisp and golden. Drain on kitchen paper and season with salt. Repeat for the remaining nests. Set aside.

3 Place a saucepan over a low heat, add the oil and butter, and slowly sweat the leeks, onion, and celery until softened. Add the herbs and potatoes, and cook for 5–6 minutes over a medium-low heat. Add the stock and bring to the boil. Reduce the heat and simmer for 30–40 minutes, until the potatoes have softened. Remove from the heat, and lift out the herbs.

4 Using a hand-held blender, blend until smooth. Add the double cream, season with salt and pepper, and blend again to combine. Serve topped with the potato nests, sliced chives, and a drizzle of leek oil.

MAKE IT *extraordinary*

A drizzle of leek oil adds a burst of colour and concentrated leek flavour to the soup.

Spiralized potatoes are deep-fried in a pea ladle to give them their neat, rounded shape.

PREP 15 MINUTES, PLUS DRAINING
COOK 1 HOUR
SERVES 4

TIM ANDERSON MasterChef Champion 2011

GAZPACHO GRANITA

This garlicky tomato soup, traditionally served cold, is an Andalusian staple. Frozen into granita and scooped into individual glasses, it makes for a refreshing summer starter. Top the granita with diced cucumber for extra colour, if you like.

1 large slice of white bread, crusts removed

150g (5½oz) roasted piquillo peppers from a jar

½ small onion, chopped

2 garlic cloves

½ cucumber, peeled, seeded, and roughly chopped

3 large ripe tomatoes on the vine, skinned and deseeded

6 whole blanched almonds, toasted in a dry pan

1 tsp salt

500ml (16fl oz) tomato juice

1 tbsp chopped parsley

100ml (3½fl oz) olive oil

1 Soak the bread in cold water for 1 minute, then squeeze out the excess moisture. This helps it to blend into the soup and thicken it. Add the bread to a blender with the remaining ingredients and blitz until smooth, in batches if necessary. Pour the soup into a shallow container and refrigerate until thoroughly chilled.

2 Check the seasoning, then stir well to blend in the olive oil, which will have risen to the top.

3 Freeze the gazpacho for 4–5 hours. Once an hour, stir and scrape the mixture with a fork to crystallize it. It should be frozen completely solid before serving. Serve in glasses or small bowls.

Roasted piquillo peppers have a mild, sweet taste, and lack the heat of other pepper varieties.

Instead of chilling gazpacho, freeze the soup into crystals to make a cooling savoury granita.

PREP 30 MINUTES, PLUS FREEZING
SERVES 4

SIMON WOOD
Champion 2015

My name is Simon Wood and I won *MasterChef* in 2015. Following my time on the show, I opened my first restaurant, Wood Manchester, in 2017, where we offer modern interpretations on traditional flavours.

What's your favourite moment from your time on the show?

My favourite moment from my time on *MasterChef* definitely has to be the team challenge day when I led my team to victory over the other one, cooking for the Red Arrows in the process. I'm a bit of an aeroplane fan so that was perfect for me.

What was the first recipe you really made your own?

The first dish that I really made my own was my wild mushroom raviolo, which is a singular, pie-like giant raviolo that is stuffed with a fricassée of wild mushrooms, chestnuts, and mascarpone, served in a sage butter sauce, with pangritata and deep-fried crispy sage leaves. It's a dish that I made before the show, one that I made on the show, and a one that I make in my restaurants now. In fact, it's our most popular starter.

Best meal of the day: breakfast, lunch, or dinner?

Best meal of the day for me is dinner because you can have wine with it, and that's frowned upon at breakfast.

What's your favourite ingredient or kitchen tool?

I'm one of those people who enjoys any type of food – there's nothing in the world that I don't like. I like mushrooms and beetroot, so I guess truffle is a favourite – I really enjoy those earthy flavours. As for my favourite piece of kitchen equipment, that has to be my chef's knife. It's essential, it comes everywhere with me.

Who is your biggest food hero, and why?

There's a couple, truth be told, but if I had to pick a stand-out food hero it's going to be Marco Pierre White. His dishes are classics, you can take inspiration from them, you only have to look at them to know how good he is, and you know what you can aspire to become.

Any advice for potential MasterChefs?

Don't be scared of trying new things – it's the only way you get better. And practise. You can practise a million times over and you're still not going to get it right, so you go again and you just practise and practise and practise.

FRENCH ONION
RAREBIT SOUP

Put a twist on this classic soup with some of the best features of a Welsh rarebit. The soup is flavoured with stout to give it depth, while the traditional cheese-topped croûton is boosted by mustard and spring onion.

Choose a rich stout, such as Guinness, to enhance the soup.

30g (1oz) butter

1 tbsp sunflower oil

675g (1½lb) onions, thinly sliced

1 tsp sugar

salt and freshly ground black pepper

2 tbsp plain white flour

1 litre (2 pints) beef stock

500ml (16fl oz) stout

115g (4oz) Gruyère or Emmental cheese, grated

2 egg yolks

1 spring onion, finely chopped

1 tsp mustard powder

1 garlic clove, cut in half

4 slices of baguette, about 2cm (¾in) thick, toasted

1 Melt the butter with the oil in a large, heavy-based saucepan over a low heat. Stir in the onions and sugar and season with salt and pepper. Press a piece of wet greaseproof paper over the surface and cook uncovered, stirring occasionally, for 40 minutes, or until the onions are rich and dark golden brown. Take care that they do not stick and burn.

2 Remove the paper, then increase the heat to medium and cook, stirring, for 5 minutes, or until the onions are glazed. Sprinkle with the flour and continue to cook, stirring, for another 2 minutes. Stir in the stock and stout and bring to the boil. Reduce the heat to low, cover, and leave the soup to simmer for 50 minutes. Taste and adjust the seasoning, if necessary.

3 Meanwhile, to make the rarebit topping, mix the cheese with the egg yolks, spring onion, and mustard powder. Preheat the grill on its highest setting. Divide the soup between 4 flameproof bowls and stir 1 tbsp brandy into each.

4 Rub the garlic clove over the toast slices. Spread the cheese mixture onto the slices and place 1 slice in each bowl. Grill for 2-3 minutes, or until the cheese is bubbling and golden. Serve at once.

Spring onions add a gentle bite to the cheese croûtons, and a bit of crunch.

PREP 10 MINUTES
COOK 1 HOUR 40 MINUTES
SERVES 4

ASPARAGUS SOUP
WITH CRISPY DUCK EGG

A deep-fried duck egg and crunchy pancetta crisps lend a vibrant pop of colour and plenty of texture to this smooth and creamy spring soup.

Soft-yolked duck eggs are deep-fried for an unusual accompaniment to this soup.

Create intensely flavoured "crisps" by baking pancetta strips between two trays.

1 litre (1¾ pints) chicken stock

salt and freshly ground black pepper

60g (2oz) butter

500g (1lb 2oz) white or green asparagus, trimmed, peeled (reserve the trimmings), and cut into 2.5cm (1in) lengths

300ml (10fl oz) milk

30g (1oz) plain flour

pinch of caster sugar

pinch of freshly grated nutmeg

2 egg yolks

2 tbsp whipping cream

3 duck eggs, 1 beaten

100g (3½oz) plain flour

150g (5½oz) fine white or Panko breadcrumbs

oil, for deep-frying and baking

8 pancetta slices

1 Combine the stock, 1 tsp salt, 20g (¾oz) of butter, and the asparagus trimmings in a saucepan. Bring to the boil, cover, and simmer for 15 minutes over a medium heat. Strain the stock and discard the trimmings, then return to the pan. Bring to the boil, and add the trimmed asparagus (retaining 4 spears). Return to the boil, cover, and cook for 10–12 minutes or until the asparagus is al dente. Strain again, reserving the asparagus and stock. Add enough milk to the stock to make 1 litre (1¾ pints).

2 Melt the remaining butter in a pan. Add the flour and cook over a low heat, stirring, for 2–3 minutes or until smooth. Gradually add the liquid, whisking vigorously to avoid lumps. Bring to the boil and cook over a low heat for 5 minutes, stirring occasionally. Add the sugar and nutmeg, then season.

3 Stir the egg yolks into the cream. Slowly add this to the soup, stirring carefully to get a smooth texture. Add the asparagus and keep warm until ready to serve. Do not boil.

4 Boil 2 duck eggs for 7 minutes. Refresh under cold running water, then carefully remove the shells. Roll the eggs in the flour, beaten duck egg, and breadcrumbs, then deep-fry them at 180°C (350°F) until golden brown.

5 Meanwhile, brush the pancetta with a little oil, then place between 2 pieces of baking parchment on a baking tray. Top with another baking tray and bake in the oven at 180°C (350°F/Gas 4) for 10 minutes. Reserve the fat. Shave the reserved asparagus into strips. Serve the soup topped with asparagus strips, pancetta crisps, and a drizzle of pancetta fat. Halve the duck eggs and serve alongside.

PREP 10 MINUTES
COOK 40 MINUTES
SERVES 4

HOT-SMOKED SALMON QUENELLES

The hot-smoked salmon gives this pâté a deep smoky flavour. Served on top of the prawns, it creates wonderful theatre as an extraordinary canapé or starter. Be brave and eat the prawn heads – they are delicious!

125ml (4fl oz) double cream

75g (2½oz) plain yogurt

200g (7oz) hot-smoked salmon

juice and finely grated zest of 1 lemon

2 tsp finely grated horseradish root

pinch of table salt

8 king prawns, cooked, heads on, and butterflied (see p244)

micro herbs, to garnish

1 Place the cream, yogurt, salmon, lemon zest and juice, horseradish, and salt in a food processor and blend until just combined.

2 Cover and place the mixture in the fridge for at least 2 hours to firm up.

3 Lay the butterflied prawns across large serving spoons. Use two dessert spoons to shape scoops of pâté into quenelles, placing each quenelle on top of a prawn.

4 For added drama, place some smoking wood chips on a platter, cover with a bit of foil, then arrange a layer of clean leaves to create a smoky woodland effect. Place the spoons on top, garnish with micro herbs, and serve.

(see p244)

MAKE IT
extraordinary

Grated horseradish root gives the pâté its peppery tang.

Moist, flaky hot-smoked salmon creates a rich pâté.

PREP 10 MINUTES, PLUS CHILLING
SERVES 8

TEA-SMOKED SCALLOPS WITH WILD GARLIC

This is a dish I cook regularly on the barbecue, but this wok-based method works just as well. Take care not to over-smoke the scallops – they only need a few minutes to take on the flavour of the tea.

12 king scallops, cleaned, in the half-shell

1 carrot, peeled and chopped into 3mm (⅛in) cubes

1 celery stalk, trimmed and chopped into 3mm (⅛in) cubes

½ onion, peeled and chopped into 3mm (⅛in) cubes

100ml (3½fl oz) white wine

50g (1¾oz) salted butter

1 tbsp chopped wild garlic leaves, plus extra to garnish

mixed fresh seaweed, to serve

FOR SMOKING

100g (3½oz) plain uncooked rice

1 tbsp loose-leaf black tea

1 tbsp caster sugar

1 Place the smoking ingredients in a wok and cover them with a layer of foil. Place a small baking dish, or a steamer rack lined with baking parchment, in the wok, making sure there is an air gap between the foil and the dish. Remove the scallops from their shells (see p245), reserving the shells. Put the scallops, including any roe, onto the dish or rack, then set the wok over a moderate heat. When it starts to smoke, cover the top of the wok with foil or a lid to seal in the smoke. Leave for about 3 minutes, until the scallops are just browned by the smoke. Remove from the heat, then carefully lift the scallops onto a plate and set aside.

2 Preheat the oven to 180°C (350°F/Gas 4). Add the carrot, celery, onion, wine, and 100ml (3½fl oz) of water to a small saucepan. Bring to a low simmer and cook for about 15 minutes, until the liquid has reduced by half. Remove from the heat.

3 On a large baking tray, lay out the shells, using pieces of crushed foil to hold them upright and steady. Into each shell add a teaspoon of the vegetable mixture and a teaspoon of its liquor, before placing a scallop on top.

4 Heat the butter in a saucepan over a moderate heat until it foams. When the foaming reduces and the butter starts to brown, remove from the heat and add the wild garlic leaves. Spoon the brown butter and wild garlic over the scallops.

5 Bake the scallops in the oven for 8 minutes, until they are cooked and spring back when touched. Serve in the shell, using the seaweed to balance the shells on the plate, and garnish with wild garlic leaves.

PREP 25 MINUTES
COOK 30 MINUTES
SERVES 4

MAKE IT *extraordinary*

Choose a tea with a deep, fragrant flavour profile: this will enrich the smoke you create.

Also known as bear's garlic or ramsons, wild garlic leaves have a delicate, chive-like flavour.

PRAWN COCKTAIL
TACOS

Update a 1970s dinner party classic by serving a fresh prawn cocktail mix in soft tortillas. If you have the time, buy raw, shell-on prawns and cook them while still in their shells – the shell is where all the flavour is. That little bit of extra effort makes a big difference.

400g (1lb) raw prawns, shells on
150ml (5fl oz) mayonnaise
4 tbsp tomato ketchup
1 tsp tomato purée
2–3 tsp Worcestershire sauce
2–3 tsp creamed horseradish
salt and freshly ground black pepper
splash of Tabasco
lemon juice, to taste
12 soft corn tortillas
1 head of gem lettuce, shredded
handful of pea shoots
2 green chillies, sliced
1 avocado, sliced (see p243)
handful of fresh coriander leaves

1 Cook the prawns in a grill pan over a medium-high heat until the shells start to char, then set aside to until cool enough to handle. Peel and devein them (see p244), then set aside.

2 In a large bowl, combine the mayonnaise, ketchup, tomato purée, Worcestershire sauce, and horseradish. Season and add the Tabasco and lemon juice to taste. Add the peeled prawns and stir until they are fully coated by the sauce.

3 To serve, layer a few prawns on each tortilla. Top with the lettuce, pea shoots, green chillies, and avocado, and garnish with coriander.

MAKE IT
extraordinary

Cool, creamy slices of avocado balance the hot chillies in this Mexican-inspired twist.

Pair tender pea shoots with crunchy lettuce to make a fresh salad for the tacos.

PREP 15 MINUTES
COOK 5 MINUTES
MAKES 12

SALMON TARTARE WITH DILL AND HOLLANDAISE

Instead of poaching salmon, try serving it tartare. The vinegar sauce lightly pickles and cooks the fish without masking its flavour, which is enhanced by dill and a rich, buttery hollandaise.

This dish demands the absolute freshest salmon you can get.

750g (1lb 10oz) skinless salmon fillet

120ml (4fl oz) white wine vinegar

2 tbsp finely chopped dill, and a few extra sprigs to serve

1 tbsp finely chopped capers, plus extra whole capers to serve

juice and grated zest of ½ lemon

sea salt and freshly ground black pepper

extra virgin olive oil, to garnish

FOR THE HOLLANDAISE

250g (9oz) unsalted butter

4 large egg yolks

1 tbsp lemon juice

1 Thinly slice the salmon fillet into 3 layers, then slice across and lengthways, to make cubes of about 5mm (¼in).

2 In a small saucepan, heat the vinegar, dill, and chopped capers, and simmer for about 5 minutes, until the liquid has reduced by half. Leave to cool.

3 To make the hollandaise, melt the butter over a low heat. Put the egg yolks and lemon juice in a blender, season, and process briefly. With the motor running, pour in the melted butter drop by drop, accelerating to a thin stream, until the mixture emulsifies into a thick sauce.

4 Combine the salmon and the cooled vinegar mixture. Add the lemon juice and zest, and then season to taste with salt and pepper.

5 To serve, place a pastry ring on each plate and fill with a generous amount of the salmon mixture. Remove the rings and add drizzles of olive oil, dollops of the hollandaise, and a scattering of capers and dill.

Dill always pairs well with fish, and especially with the near-raw salmon in this dish.

Choose capers stored in brine to match the tart taste of the vinegar dressing.

PREP 10 MINUTES, PLUS COOLING
COOK 10 MINUTES
SERVES 4

SEAFOOD TEMPURA WITH WASABI MAYO

Light, crunchy parcels filled with tender fish and seafood are accompanied by a tangy wasabi mayonnaise made extra special by the addition of lumpfish caviar.

A spoonful of caviar gives the mayonnaise a salty tang to match the seafood.

Wasabi (also known as Japanese horseradish) adds a fiery kick to the mayonnaise.

FOR THE BATTER
60g (2oz) cornflour
225g (8oz) self-raising flour
1/4 tsp ground turmeric
3/4 tsp salt
600ml (1 pint) cold beer
  (not dark)

FOR THE SEAFOOD
oil, for deep frying
175g (6oz) white fish fillet,
  pin-boned and skinned
115g (4oz) raw tiger prawns,
  peeled and deveined
8 scallops
2 squid, gutted, cleaned, and
  cut into rings
salt and freshly ground black
  pepper

FOR THE WASABI MAYONNAISE
5 tbsp Japanese mayonnaise,
  such as Kewpie
3/4 tbsp wasabi powder
1 tbsp clear plum sauce
1 tbsp lumpfish caviar

1 To make the tempura batter, put the cornflour and self-raising flour, turmeric, and salt in a bowl. Slowly add the beer, and whisk together to combine. Cover and place in the fridge to chill for 20–30 minutes.

2 Mix together the ingredients for the wasabi mayonnaise. Set aside until ready to serve.

3 Heat the oil in a deep-fat fryer or a small saucepan to 180°C (350°F). Dip the prepared fish, shellfish, and squid in the batter a few pieces at a time, and fry until they are crisp but still quite pale in colour. Drain on kitchen paper.

4 Season the tempura with salt and pepper, and serve with the wasabi mayonnaise on the side for dipping.

PREP 10 MINUTES,
PLUS CHILLING
COOK 20 MINUTES
SERVES 4

CRAB SALAD WITH MINT AND POMELO

A delicate crab salad unlike any other: slices of pomelo, finely sliced radish, fragrant mint leaves, and a light lime dressing combine to make a fresh, citrussy dish that works well served with a side of baby salad leaves.

350g (12oz) cooked fresh or canned white crabmeat, drained

4 radishes, finely sliced

handful of coriander leaves

handful of mint leaves

1 pomelo, peeled, segmented, pith removed (see p242)

micro amaranth, to garnish (optional)

FOR THE DRESSING

3 tbsp rapeseed oil

juice of 2 limes

pinch of unrefined golden caster sugar

sea salt, to taste

1 In a small bowl or jug, whisk together the dressing ingredients. Season with salt to taste.

2 Mix the crabmeat with a drizzle of the dressing. Divide the radish slices, coriander leaves, and mint leaves between 4 serving plates. Scatter over the pomelo segments.

3 When ready to serve, drizzle the salad with the remaining dressing. Divide the crabmeat mixture between the plates, spooning it on neatly or shaping it as you wish. Scatter with micro amaranth, if using, and serve immediately.

MAKE IT
extraordinary

Cool mint leaves will offset the salad's tart citrus flavours and the peppery crunch of radish.

The pomelo is a citrus fruit, similar to a grapefruit, but with slightly sweeter flesh.

PREP 10 MINUTES
SERVES 4

ALL-DAY BREAKFAST CAESAR SALAD

This twist on the classic Italian–American salad features some of the best components of a full English breakfast – crisp bacon, black pudding, and pickled quail eggs – to pick up on the salt-sour vinaigrette of the Caesar's traditional anchovy dressing.

1 tbsp olive oil

6 rashers streaky bacon, sliced

200g (7oz) black pudding, diced

2 stale brioche buns, cubed

2 small heads of Cos lettuce, torn into small pieces

60g (2oz) Parmesan cheese, shaved

6 pickled quail eggs

FOR THE DRESSING

2 garlic cloves

2 anchovy fillets in olive oil, drained and finely chopped

1 tbsp fresh lemon juice

1 tsp Worcestershire sauce

120ml (4fl oz) extra virgin olive oil

freshly ground black pepper

1 Heat the olive oil in a frying pan over a medium heat. Add the bacon lardons and black pudding and fry until golden and crispy. Remove with a slotted spoon and set aside on kitchen paper. Add the brioche cubes to the pan and fry in the bacon fat until golden, then drain on kitchen paper.

2 To make the dressing, mash the garlic and anchovies together in a pestle and mortar to make a thick paste. Transfer to a screw-top jar, add the extra virgin olive oil, lemon juice, and Worcestershire sauce. Shake the dressing until well blended, then season to taste with pepper. Set aside.

3 To assemble the salad, toss the lettuce leaves, bacon lardons, black pudding, and brioche croutons in a large salad bowl. Halve the quail eggs and add to the bowl. Shake the dressing again, then add to the salad, and toss again. Sprinkle with the Parmesan shavings and serve at once.

MAKE IT *extraordinary*

Fry strips of streaky bacon until crisp to give the salad plenty of texture.

Black pudding is classic part of any fried breakfast. Swap for more bacon if you prefer.

Pickled quail eggs replace plain boiled eggs, adding a sourness to balance the salty bacon.

PREP 10 MINUTES
COOK 10 MINUTES
SERVES 6

WARM MADRAS CHICKEN SALAD

The addition of Madras curry paste and coconut milk, a bed of colourful radicchio, carrot, and spinach, and a spiced dressing gives this classic chicken salad a gentle kick.

FOR THE CHICKEN
4 chicken breasts, skin on, each about 150g (5½oz)
4 tsp Madras curry paste
4 tbsp coconut milk
1 tsp salt
2 tbsp vegetable oil

FOR THE SALAD
¼ small red cabbage, thinly sliced
1 small head of radicchio, torn into small pieces
2 carrots, julienned
200g (7oz) baby spinach
4 poppadums

FOR THE SPICED DRESSING
4 tbsp crème fraîche
1 tsp Madras curry paste
juice of 1 lemon
2 tbsp olive oil
salt and freshly ground black pepper

1 Lay a chicken breast in between 2 sheets of cling film and flatten gently with a rolling pin. Repeat with the other 3 breasts. This allows the chicken breasts to cook quickly and retain their moisture.

2 Mix the curry paste, coconut milk, and salt together in a bowl, and marinate the chicken breasts for at least 30 minutes, or overnight if possible.

3 Heat a frying pan with the oil, lay each breast skin-side down, and fry over a medium heat for 4-5 minutes. Flip and cook the other side for 3-4 minutes, until the chicken is cooked through. Set aside.

4 While the chicken is cooking, combine all the salad ingredients, except for the poppadums, in a large bowl and mix well. Divide the salad between 4 individual bowls.

5 Combine the ingredients for the spiced dressing in a bowl and season to taste with salt and pepper.

6 Slice the chicken and place on top of each salad, then add dollops of spiced dressing. Break the poppadums into shards and nestle these in among the salad.

MAKE IT *extraordinary*

Marinating the chicken overnight in coconut milk gives it a rich, sweet flavour.

Madras curry paste adds spice to both the marinade and the creamy dressing.

PREP 15 MINUTES, PLUS MARINATING
COOK 10 MINUTES
SERVES 4

SAFFRON EGGS BENEDICT WITH SPINACH

With a layer of rich creamed spinach and a cheesy saffron hollandaise sauce, this updated brunch classic deserves to be served with a glass of champagne.

60g (2oz) butter
pinch of saffron threads
30g (1oz) plain flour
300ml (10fl oz) warm milk
salt and freshly ground black pepper
4 eggs and 2 egg yolks
2 tbsp double cream
½ tsp wholegrain English mustard
70g (2½oz) Gruyère cheese, grated
70g (2½oz) Comté cheese, grated
splash of vinegar or lemon juice
1 banana shallot, finely chopped
450g (1lb) fresh spinach
1–1½ tsp chopped tarragon
½–1 tsp chopped parsley
2 English muffins, halved, toasted, and buttered
4 slices smoked ham

1 Melt half the butter in a small saucepan with the saffron, stir in the flour, and cook for 1 minute. Remove the pan from the heat and gradually beat in the milk. Return to the heat and cook, stirring, until the sauce thickens. Season to taste with salt and pepper. Whisk in the 2 egg yolks, cream, and mustard, then add the cheeses, and stir until melted. Keep warm.

2 Poach the eggs (see p246). Lift out and drain briefly on kitchen paper.

3 Melt the remaining butter in a large saucepan and fry the shallot over a medium heat for 2–3 minutes, or until softened. Add the spinach, cover, and cook for a few minutes until wilted, then drain well and stir through the tarragon and parsley. Preheat the grill to its highest setting.

4 Place the prepared muffins on a baking tray. Spread each with a little of the cheese sauce, then lay a slice of ham on top. Spread the ham with a little more sauce, then top each one with some spinach.

5 Place a poached egg on top of the spinach and pour over a generous amount of the sauce. Place under the grill until the sauce starts to bubble and turn golden. Remove from the grill and place on serving plates. Serve with a glass of champagne.

MAKE IT *extraordinary*

Saffron not only gives the sauce a distinctive flavour, but also its golden colour.

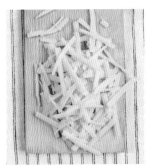

Grated Gruyère and Comté transform rich hollandaise into a tangy cheese sauce.

PREP 10 MINUTES
COOK 10 MINUTES
SERVES 4

ANCHO CHILLI
PULLED PORK CANAPÉS

Turn slow-cooked pulled pork into a hands-on starter
with freshly made guacamole and homemade nachos,
made by deep-frying fresh tortilla wraps.

2kg (4½lb) bone-in pork
   shoulder
sea salt
4-6 tortilla wraps
oil, for deep-frying
shredded lettuce, sliced red
   onion, cherry tomatoes, and
   coriander, to serve

FOR THE SAUCE

2 tbsp sunflower oil, plus extra
   for rubbing
4 large rehydrated ancho
   chillies, chopped
1 onion, finely chopped
2 garlic cloves, crushed
100ml (3½fl oz) tomato ketchup
4 tbsp cider vinegar
1 tsp Tabasco or other hot sauce
1 tsp Worcestershire sauce
1 tsp dried mustard powder
2 tbsp runny honey
50g (1¾oz) dark chocolate
   (85 per cent), finely grated

GUACAMOLE

2 ripe, soft avocados, halved
   lengthways, stone removed
   (see p243)
1 red chilli, deseeded and
   finely chopped
2 tbsp finely chopped fresh
   coriander
1 tsp smoked paprika
freshly ground white pepper
zest and juice of 2 limes

1 Prepare the sauce. Heat the oil in a small, heavy-based
pan. Fry the onion over a medium heat for 5 minutes until
softened. Add the garlic and fry for 1 minute. Add the remaining
ingredients, except for the chocolate, with 100ml (3½fl oz) of
water and whisk well. Bring to the boil then simmer, uncovered,
for 20 minutes until reduced to a thick sauce. Remove from
the heat and add the chocolate, then blend until smooth using
a hand-held blender. Set aside to cool. Rub the sauce into the
pork, cover, and chill for at least 4 hours, preferably overnight.

2 Preheat the oven to 180°C (350°F/Gas 4). Place the pork
and sauce in an oven tray just big enough to fit it. Cover
with a piece of greaseproof paper and seal with a double layer
of foil. Cook the pork for 2½ hours, then remove from the
oven and increase the temperature to 230°C (450°F/Gas 8).

3 Strain off the sauce into a pan and skim off the fat. Rub
the pork with a little oil and season with sea salt. Return
the pork to the oven and cook, uncovered, for 30 minutes,
until the crackling is crisp. Remove the crackling and leave
uncovered. Wrap the meat in foil and rest it for 10 minutes.

4 Meanwhile, reduce the sauce over a medium heat to a
thick pouring consistency. Cut the tortillas into triangles
and deep fry at 190°C (375°F) until golden.

5 For the guacamole, scoop out the avocado flesh into a
bowl and mash with a fork. Mix through the remaining
ingredients until smooth and evenly combined. To serve,
shred the pork with two forks and divide between plates.
Pour over some of the sauce, and serve with a few nachos,
guacamole, the remaining sauce, and salad.

Ancho chillies are dried poblano
peppers. They can be sourced
from larger supermarkets.

Choose dark chocolate with
a high cocoa content – ideally
85 per cent.

Crunchy, deep-fried homemade
nachos will rival shop-bought
corn varieties.

PREP 30 MINUTES,
PLUS CHILLING
COOK 3 HOURS 30 MINUTES
SERVES 4-6

FISH AND SEAFOOD

THAI RED CURRY FISH CAKES

As well as the inclusion of Thai red curry ingredients, this recipe uses a traditional Thai process to beat the mixture together, resulting in a light and airy texture.

200g (7oz) cod fillet

3 tbsp fish sauce

2 tbsp palm sugar or light brown muscovado

1 egg yolk

4 makrut (kaffir) lime leaves, finely shredded

1 tbsp finely shredded coriander leaves

3-4 tbsp vegetable oil or sunflower oil

sweet chilli sauce, to serve

rocket leaves, to garnish

FOR THE CURRY PASTE

4 dried red Thai chillies, soaked in water

2 tbsp finely diced red shallots

3 tbsp crushed garlic

2 tbsp finely sliced lemongrass

2 tsp finely chopped coriander root, or coriander stems

4 makrut (kaffir) lime leaves, finely sliced

½ tsp shrimp paste

1 Put all the paste ingredients into a food processor and blitz until you have a thick paste, adding a little water if needed. Set aside.

2 Finely slice the cod. Place into a large bowl and beat against the side of the bowl with a spoon. Continue to do this until it starts to get sticky and mousse-like. This can take up to 5 minutes. Add the fish sauce and sugar and continue to beat to incorporate.

3 When the fish reaches a mousse-like consistency, add 3 tbsp of the red curry paste and mix thoroughly, then stir in the egg yolk, lime leaves, and coriander leaves. Reserve the remaining red curry paste for another recipe.

4 Heat a little of the oil in a frying pan over a medium-high heat. For each fish cake, scoop up a tablespoon of the mixture, then carefully slide it into the pan and flatten to about 2cm (¾in) thick. Shallow fry the fish cakes for 1-2 minutes on each side, until golden, in batches if necessary. Drain on kitchen paper.

5 Serve the fish cakes hot, with sweet chilli sauce for dipping and a garnish of rocket leaves.

MAKE IT *extraordinary*

Homemade Thai red curry paste, made with fresh lemongrass, gives the fish cakes a kick.

Makrut, or kaffir, lime leaves are used in many Thai dishes to add an aromatic, lemon-lime flavour.

PREP TIME 15 MINUTES
COOK TIME 15 MINUTES
SERVES 4

BAKED HALIBUT IN A NUTTY COUSCOUS CRUST

Rosemary- and garlic-flavoured couscous combined with a beurre noisette and chopped nuts makes an extra crunchy, buttery crumb coating for delicate halibut fillets in this baked dish.

MAKE IT
extraordinary

Use crunchy couscous instead of breadcrumbs as a base for the halibut's crust.

60g (2oz) couscous

125g (4½oz) butter

juice of 1 lemon

1 tsp turmeric

1 tbsp chopped rosemary leaves, plus extra sprigs to garnish

1 large garlic clove, grated or finely chopped

60g (2oz) pecorino or Parmesan cheese, finely grated

100g (3½oz) pistachio nuts, chopped

100g (3½oz) pine nuts, chopped

salt and freshly ground black pepper

sunflower oil, for greasing

1 egg, beaten

3 tbsp seasoned flour

4 halibut fillets, about 150g (5½oz) each

200ml (7fl oz) passata

½ tsp clear honey

1 Preheat the oven to 190°C (375°F/Gas 5). Place the couscous in a bowl and stir in 75ml (2½ fl oz) boiling water. Cover and leave for 5 minutes, then spread on a plate and leave to cool.

2 Make a beurre noisette by melting the butter in a small saucepan over a medium heat until there are large bubbles and the butter starts to brown, then add the lemon juice and remove from the heat.

3 Stir in the turmeric, chopped rosemary, and garlic. Mix in the couscous, followed by the cheese, pistachios, and pine nuts, and season with salt and pepper. Oil a roasting tin and place it in the oven to heat up.

4 Put the egg on one plate, and the flour on another. Dip the fish in the flour, then the egg, then the couscous mixture. Put it in the hot roasting tin. Bake for 15 minutes until golden and cooked through, turning once.

5 Meanwhile, heat the passata and honey together in a pan. Season to taste. Spoon onto 4 warmed plates and top with the halibut. Garnish with sprigs of rosemary and serve with baby potatoes and French beans.

Pistachios add a delicate hint of green to the couscous crust.

Pine nuts give the crust a noticeable crunch that contrasts with the flaky halibut fillets.

PREP 20 MINUTES
COOK 15 MINUTES
SERVES 4

MAT FOLLAS
Champion 2009

I'm Mat Follas and I won *MasterChef* in 2009. The show has been a wonderful springboard for my food career, and I've since written three cookbooks and opened two restaurants: The Wild Garlic and Bramble Café.

Q What's your favourite moment from your time on the show and why?

A It was when I went to a restaurant called Noma, which I'd never heard of at the time, and it has since become the number-one restaurant in the world. I was really into foraging and finding wild plants. I'd used them a couple of times on the show, but hadn't thought of them as fine dining or good enough for *MasterChef*. But a few days at Noma completely changed my way of thinking. I brought that knowledge into the final and I believe it's the reason I won.

Q What was your worst kitchen moment?

A When I was making some sweet chilli sauce and forgot about it. My restaurant was on a little square. I had wandered across to the butcher and could smell it burning from the other side of the square.

Q What was the first recipe you really made your own?

A I think it was something as simple as making scones. I used to really enjoy baking. I lived on my own from about the age of 16, and I used to bake my own bread and make my own cakes.

Q What's your favourite kitchen tool and why?

A My favourite tool is a stick blender. You can do so many things with it - making sauces, even cakes in an emergency.

Q Who is your biggest food hero and why?

A It has to be Rene Redzepi at Noma. His food is just extraordinary, and there is always something new coming through. It gives chefs and cooks that ability to experiment, as he's always pushing those boundaries for us.

Q Best meal of the day: breakfast, lunch, or dinner?

A It's got to be brunch. At the café we do a brunch with bubble and squeak and bacon. I wouldn't have my figure if it wasn't for that brunch.

Q Any advice for potential MasterChefs?

A It's not glamorous. Don't do it unless you really love cooking, and you don't mind working damn hard. The pay's rubbish, but it's a great job, and I love it.

OVEN-BAKED SEA BASS WITH PISTOU SOUP

Sea bass is a delicious, delicate fish, which is given a twist with the addition of Provençal pistou. Get your fishmonger to prepare the fish for you and don't forget the bones for the stock. This dish is great for dinner parties, as you can prepare up to step 2 in advance.

Samphire brings a salty, seaside flavour to the pistou.

4 bass fillets, skinned and boned

FOR THE SOUP
2 carrots, finely chopped
2 celery sticks, finely sliced
1 onion, finely chopped
25ml (1fl oz) Pernod
bones from 2 x 1kg (2¼lb) bass,
   heads removed

FOR THE PISTOU
1 garlic clove, finely diced
1 carrot, finely diced
1 celery stick, finely diced
3 tbsp olive oil
100g (3½oz) samphire, picked
   and chopped into 3mm (⅛in)
   pieces
small bunch of parsley, finely
   chopped
leaves from 10-12 chervil sprigs

1 Place all the soup ingredients in a large saucepan and bring to a low simmer. Simmer for 15 minutes, then remove from the heat and set aside to infuse for 45 minutes. Strain the soup into a saucepan, using a muslin cloth for the best results, and discard the bones and stock vegetables.

2 Meanwhile, to make the pistou, place the garlic, carrot, celery, and a dash of olive oil in a small saucepan. Cook over a very low heat for about 20 minutes, until soft. Remove the saucepan from the heat and fold in the remaining pistou ingredients, adding just enough oil to hold the mixture together.

3 Preheat the oven to 140°C (275°F/Gas 1). Place the fillets on a baking tray lined with baking parchment and bake for 10 minutes, until the fish is just cooked.

4 Heat up the soup. Warm 4 soup bowls and add a generous bed of pistou to each bowl. Place a sea bass fillet on top. To serve, fill a jug or gravy boat with the soup and pour it over the fish at the table.

PREP 15 MINUTES,
PLUS INFUSING
COOK 35 MINUTES
SERVES 4

PIPI SOUP

This alternative to clam chowder features pipis, a large variety of clam native to New Zealand. The additional hints of ginger and soy in this recipe reflect the strong influence of Chinese immigration in the country.

100ml (3½fl oz) white wine

1.5kg (3lb 3oz) Pipi clams

50g (1¾oz) edible dried seaweed

2 leeks, thinly sliced

2 onions, finely chopped

10 new potatoes, halved

30g (1oz) fresh root ginger, grated

2 tsp dark soy sauce

1 Place the wine and 200ml (7fl oz) water in a large saucepan and bring to a simmer. Carefully place the clams in the saucepan, cover, and return to the heat for a few minutes, until the clams open. Meanwhile, place the dried seaweed in another saucepan.

2 When the clams are ready, strain off the liquid and pour it over the seaweed. Set the clams aside. Simmer the seaweed gently for 10 minutes, until fully rehydrated. Strain the stock and reserve for the soup. Set the seaweed aside until ready to serve.

3 Add the leeks, onions, and potatoes to a saucepan, cover with water, and boil until the potatoes are cooked. Drain and set aside half the vegetables, reserving some cooking water.

4 Add the other half of the vegetables to the seaweed stock and blitz with a hand-held blender until the mixture reaches the consistency of double cream, adding some of the vegetable cooking water if required. Bring to a low simmer, add the ginger and soy sauce, and season to taste.

5 Divide the seaweed between individual soup bowls. Place the clams and remaining vegetables on top, and serve, pouring over the hot soup at the table.

MAKE IT
extraordinary

Pipis lend their name to this soup, but you could use another large clam, such as Venus clams.

Dried seaweed is sold in Asian supermarkets, and complements the taste of the shellfish.

PREP 15 MINUTES
COOK 30 MINUTES
SERVES 4

SUMAC TROUT WITH CUMIN AND ALMONDS

This dish combines two classic flavour combinations: the French-inspired trout amandine, or trout with flaked almonds, and Middle Eastern sumac, a spice which has long been paired with fish.

MAKE IT
extraordinary

Flaked almonds make a delicate, crunchy topping.

4 fresh trout, gutted and rinsed

2 limes, sliced into thin rounds and halved

1 tbsp ground sumac

1 tsp ground cumin

2 tbsp olive oil

60g (2oz) flaked almonds

1 tbsp finely chopped flat-leaf parsley

1 tbsp finely chopped coriander leaves

1 Preheat the oven to 200°C (400°F/Gas 6). Make 3–4 diagonal slashes about 5mm (¼in) deep on either side of each trout. Place the fish side by side in a shallow ovenproof dish. Tuck the halved lime slices into the slashes and inside the cavity. Sprinkle the sumac and cumin over and inside the fish, then drizzle over the olive oil.

2 Bake uncovered for 12 minutes, or until the fish flakes easily with a fork. Add the almonds and cook for a further 2 minutes in the oven.

3 Remove from the oven and allow the fish to rest for 5 minutes. Scatter over the chopped parsley and coriander before serving.

A sprinkle of ground sumac gives the trout an extra citrussy tang and a pop of colour.

PREP 15 MINUTES
COOK 15 MINUTES
SERVES 4

THAI-STYLE MOULES MARINIÈRES

Balance cooling coconut and lemongrass with the heat of fresh chilli in this Thai-inspired take on a French seafood classic. Garnish with coriander to complement the flavours in this dish.

60g (2oz) butter

2 onions, finely chopped

3.6kg (8lb) mussels, cleaned and debearded (see p244)

2 garlic cloves, crushed

1 lemongrass stalk, bruised

1 red chilli, finely chopped

400ml (14fl oz) dry white wine

200ml (7fl oz) coconut milk

salt and freshly ground black pepper

2–4 tbsp chopped coriander leaves, plus extra whole leaves for garnish

1 Melt the butter in a large, heavy-based saucepan. Add the onions and fry gently until lightly browned. Add the mussels, garlic, lemongrass, chilli, wine, and coconut milk. Season with salt and pepper. Cover, bring to the boil, and cook, shaking the pan frequently, for 10 minutes, or until the mussels have opened.

2 Remove the mussels with a slotted spoon, discarding any that remain closed. Transfer them to warmed bowls, cover, and keep warm.

3 Strain the liquor into a pan and bring back to the boil. Season to taste and add the chopped coriander. Pour over the mussels, garnish with whole coriander leaves, and serve at once.

MAKE IT *extraordinary*

Bruise the lemongrass with the flat of a knife to allow it to release its flavour into the liquor.

As it cooks, the chillies give a heat to the mussels.

Cooling, creamy coconut milk balances the heat of the chilli.

PREP 15 MINUTES
COOK 15 MINUTES
SERVES 4

FISH PIE WITH THE ULTIMATE MASH

Don't settle for shop-bought fish pie mix and a plain mashed potato topping. This recipe combines rich smoked mackerel, fresh salmon, and tiger prawns in a creamy sauce, topped with an unbeatably smooth and lemony celeriac–potato mash.

MAKE IT *extraordinary*

The white wine sauce will take on a smoky undertone from the mackerel.

Large, firm tiger prawns add plenty of bite to the fish pie mix.

- 2 shallots, finely chopped
- 250ml (9fl oz) white wine
- 250ml (9fl oz) double cream
- 250g (9oz) salmon fillet, skinned and cut into cubes
- 250g (9oz) un-dyed smoked mackerel, skinned and cut into cubes
- 250g (9oz) raw, peeled tiger prawns
- 1 tbsp wholegrain mustard
- 1 tbsp finely chopped flat-leaf parsley
- 1 tbsp finely chopped tarragon
- sea salt and freshly ground black pepper
- olive oil for drizzling

FOR THE MASH

- 450g (1lb) floury potatoes, peeled and quartered
- 450g (1lb) celeriac, peeled and cut into chunks
- 3 tbsp milk
- 50g (1¾oz) unsalted butter
- zest and juice of ½ lemon

1 Preheat the oven to 200°C (400°F/Gas 6). To make the mash, cook the potatoes and celeriac in a pan of boiling salted water for about 15 minutes, until soft. Drain and mash thoroughly with the milk, butter, and lemon zest and juice. Season to taste. Pass through a sieve and set aside.

2 Meanwhile, put the shallots and wine in a large saucepan and bring to the boil, then simmer until the wine has reduced by half. Add the cream and continue to simmer until the sauce coats the back of a spoon.

3 Add the salmon and mackerel to the saucepan, along with the prawns. Stir in the mustard, parsley, and tarragon, season with a pinch of salt and pepper, and cook, stirring regularly, for about 5 minutes.

4 Pour the mixture into an ovenproof dish. Spoon the mash into a piping bag fitted with a round nozzle and pipe neat rounds of mash across the surface of the pie. Drizzle with olive oil, and bake in the oven for 15–20 minutes, until the fish is cooked through and the topping is crisp and golden.

PREP 20 MINUTES
COOK 40 MINUTES
SERVES 4-6

MASALA AND YOGURT ROASTED MONKFISH

Monkfish is robust enough to take the strong flavours of this freshly made masala spice mix, which can also be used in other dishes alongside fresh ginger and garlic. I love a mild curry, but you can add extra chilli powder if you prefer more heat.

Adjust the amount of chilli powder in your masala spice mix to suit your preference.

6 monkfish fillets, skinned, 1.4kg (3lb) in total
300g (10oz) Basmati rice, to serve
bunch of coriander, to serve

FOR THE MASALA SPICE
5 tsp ground coriander
4 tsp ground cumin
2 tsp ground fenugreek
2 tsp chilli powder
1 tsp ground cardamom
1 tsp ground cloves
1 tsp ground mace

FOR THE MARINADE
250g (9oz) plain yogurt
50g (1¾oz) tomato purée
2 tsp finely grated root ginger
2 tsp crushed garlic
1 tsp salt

1 Mix the masala spice and marinade ingredients together in a bowl to make the marinade.

2 Place the marinade and the monkfish in a plastic bag, seal it, then massage the bag to thoroughly coat the fish in the marinade. Leave in the fridge for at least 6 hours.

3 Preheat the oven to 180°C (350°F/Gas 4). Line a baking tray with baking parchment. Remove the fillets from the marinade and arrange side by side on the parchment, spacing them out well. Spoon the remaining marinade over the fillets.

4 Roast the fillets in the oven, brushing occasionally with the juices in the tray, for 35–40 minutes, until the flesh just flakes when tested with a fork.

5 Serve with hot Basmati rice and garnish with a few coriander leaves.

PREP 10 MINUTES, PLUS MARINATING
COOK 40 MINUTES
SERVES 6

SAFFRON KEDGEREE WITH MACKEREL AND MUSSELS

Update this Anglo-Indian dish with saffron-infused stock and some rich seafood additions, topped with a runny, freshly poached egg.

200g (7oz) Basmati rice

pinch of saffron threads

450g (15oz) hot smoked mackerel

450g (15oz) mussels, cleaned and debearded (see p244)

60g (2oz) ghee (or 60g (2oz) butter and 30g (1oz) sunflower oil)

1 tsp ground fenugreek

½ tsp madras curry powder

1 tsp coriander seeds

1 tsp cumin seeds

1 tsp fennel seeds

4 eggs

salt and freshly ground black pepper

1 tbsp chopped parsley

1 lemon, cut into wedges (optional)

1 Cook the rice in boiling, salted water with a few saffron threads for 10-12 minutes, or according to the packet instructions. When cooked, drain and place in a bowl.

2 Flake the fish into large chunks, discarding any skin and bones. Add the fish and mussels to the rice.

3 Place the ghee in a large, heavy-based non-stick frying pan, over a moderate heat. Add the fenugreek, curry powder, coriander, cumin, and fennel and cook, stirring lightly, until the seeds begin to pop. Remove from the heat. Add the rice mixture and about 3 tbsp water, stirring to coat the rice with the spices. Cover the pan and return it to a low heat, keeping it covered until the mussels are cooked and open.

4 Poach the eggs for 5-6 minutes (see p246), until the whites are cooked but the yolks still runny.

5 While the eggs are cooking, stir the rice mixture and divide between heated plates. Place the just-poached eggs on top, season with salt and pepper, and sprinkle with chopped parsley. Serve garnished with lemon wedges, if using.

MAKE IT
extraordinary

Fresh mussels add a briny tang that contrasts with the smoky flavour of the mackerel.

You only need a small pinch of saffron to colour the rice and flavour the dish.

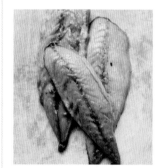

Good-quality, hot-smoked mackerel will flake into the rice and flavour the stock.

PREP 5 MINUTES
COOK 30 MINUTES
SERVES 4

CAPELLINI WITH CLAMS, COCONUT, AND CHILLI

Italian classic spaghetti alle vongole gets an Asian flavour infusion in this dish. A crispy lemon and herb crumb topping provides a contrast in texture to the delicate capellini ("angel hair") pasta.

MAKE IT
extraordinary

Coconut milk is flavoured by the clam liquor and fish stock to make a rich seafood-based sauce.

Finely chopped chilli adds a kick to the creamy coconut sauce.

3 tbsp olive oil

2 shallots, finely chopped

5 garlic cloves, thinly sliced widthways

2 red bird's-eye chillies, finely chopped

280g can clams, drained and liquor reserved

100ml (3½fl oz) fish stock

100ml (3½fl oz) coconut milk

400g (14oz) capellini pasta

chopped coriander leaves, to serve

FOR THE TOPPING

olive oil

50g (1¾oz) fresh breadcrumbs

zest of 1 lemon

2 tbsp chopped coriander leaves

2 tbsp chopped parsley

1 Heat 2 tbsp of the oil in a heavy-based saucepan and fry the shallots over a medium heat for 4–5 minutes, until softened but not browned. Add the garlic and chilli, and cook until fragrant. Pour in the clam liquor and fish stock and continue cooking until it reduces, then add the coconut milk and continue to cook until the sauce is thick enough to coat the back of a spoon. Remove from the heat and set aside.

2 Make the crumb topping. Add some oil to a small pan, and toast the breadcrumbs over a medium heat until golden brown, taking care not to let them burn. Remove from the heat and allow to cool, then stir in the lemon zest and herbs. Set aside until ready to serve.

3 Cook the capellini in a large pan of boiling salted water according to the packet instructions. Reserve a ladleful of the cooking water, then drain the pasta, and return it to the pan with the reserved water.

4 Add the clams and remaining 1 tbsp of olive oil to the sauce, and allow to heat through, before tossing with the capellini. Serve immediately, with the breadcrumb mixture and freshly chopped coriander sprinkled on top.

PREP 5 MINUTES
COOK 30 MINUTES
SERVES 4

BLACK SESAME-CRUSTED TUNA WITH PONZU AND SAMPHIRE

Black sesame seeds give this classic tuna dish an eye-catching crust, while the ponzu (Japanese dipping sauce) is packed with flavour. For an extremely luxurious variation, use sashimi-quality tuna belly.

MAKE IT
extraordinary

Nutty black sesame seeds contrast dramatically with the pink flesh of the tuna.

Fresh samphire gives a salty flavour to this dish, echoing the taste of the sea.

5 tbsp sesame oil, plus extra for searing

1 garlic clove, crushed

1 small hot red chilli, finely chopped

salt

2 tuna steaks, about 300g (10oz) each, halved lengthways

2 radishes

juice of ½ lemon

4 tbsp black sesame seeds, plus extra for garnish

200g (7oz) samphire

½ tbsp unsalted butter

FOR THE PONZU

4 tbsp Japanese soy sauce

1½ tbsp yuzu juice

1 tsp sugar

1 tsp rice vinegar

1. Rinse the tuna steaks and pat dry with kitchen paper. Mix 4 tbsp of the oil, the garlic, chilli, and a sprinkling of salt on a large flat dish. Carefully press the steaks into the mixture, then cover, and chill for at least 1 hour.

2. Meanwhile, cut the radishes into matchsticks, and put them in a bowl with the lemon juice to prevent browning.

3. Remove the tuna from the fridge 15 minutes before cooking. Press the sesame seeds onto both sides of the steaks so that they stick firmly to the marinade. Heat the remaining 1 tbsp of oil in a frying pan over a high heat. Sear the tuna for 20 seconds on each side. Leave to rest for 5 minutes.

4. Make the ponzu by stirring all the ingredients together until the sugar dissolves.

5. Boil the samphire for 1 minute. Drain well, then toss with the butter and divide between 4 plates along with the radish. Place a tuna steak on each, and serve with the ponzu on the side. Scatter over the extra sesame seeds.

PREP 20 MINUTES, PLUS MARINATING
COOKS 1 MINUTE
SERVES 4

POULTRY AND MEAT

UPSIDE-DOWN CHICKEN PIE

I can't enthuse enough about the flavour of slow-roasted chicken. This takes longer than a classic pot pie, but you can prepare up to the end of step 4 up to 2 days ahead.

1 free-range chicken, about 1.5kg (3lb 3oz)

olive oil

sea salt

600ml (1 pint) chicken stock

20g (¾oz) cornflour, dissolved in a little cold water

280g (10oz) frozen peas, thawed

2 parsnips, peeled and cut into 5mm (¼in) cubes

2 carrots, peeled and cut into 5mm (¼in) cubes

3 x 500g blocks all-butter puff pastry

1 small egg, beaten, to glaze

1 Preheat the oven to 130°C (250°F/Gas ½). Place the chicken in a flameproof roasting tin, oil and generously salt the skin, then roast for 3 hours. It is done when the skin is golden and crispy and the meat flakes off the bones when pulled gently. Increase the oven temperature to 180°C (350°F/Gas 4).

2 Pick the skin and meat off the chicken and set aside, leaving the bones and cooking juices in the tin. Add the stock to the tin and cook on the hob for about 10 minutes, until reduced by half. Strain the juices into a small pan and bring to a low simmer. Gradually add the cornflour mixture, whisking gently, until it reaches the consistency of double cream. Season and set aside.

3 Place the chicken skin on a baking tray lined with baking parchment and bake for 30 minutes, until golden and crispy. Crumble the skin and set aside. Increase the oven temperature to 200°C (400°F/Gas 6). Meanwhile, break up the meat into roughly 1cm (½in) pieces.

4 Place the vegetables in a small pan and cover with salted water. Bring to a simmer, then immediately remove from the heat, drain, and plunge into ice water. Drain again and set aside.

5 Roll out the pastry on a lightly floured surface to about 1cm (½in) thick. Cut out 8 rounds using a 15cm (6in) pastry cutter. Place 4 rounds on 2 lined baking sheets, glaze with a little beaten egg, then stick the other 4 rounds on top. Glaze with the remaining egg, then bake for 20–25 minutes, or until risen and golden. Leave to cool for a few minutes, then use a sharp knife to cut a circle in the top layer, about half the diameter of the pastry. Remove each circle and fill the holes with a few generous spoonfuls of chicken and a spoonful of vegetables then return to the oven for 5 minutes to heat through. Serve garnished with the crumbled chicken skin, with jugs of gravy alongside.

Baked puff pastry bases turn the traditonal pot pie upside down.

Crunchy chicken skin tops the pie, contrasting with the tender, slow-roasted chicken meat.

PREP 30 MINUTES
COOK 4 HOURS 15 MINUTES
SERVES 4

CHICKEN SATAY SLIDERS

Instead of skewers, serve this classic Thai chicken satay in mini burger-style sliders, with marinaded chicken patties, homemade sauce, and a tangy red slaw.

FOR THE SLIDERS

3 tbsp vegetable oil, plus extra for frying

2 lemongrass stalks, chopped

3 whole garlic cloves, peeled

2 banana shallots, chopped

2 tsp ground coriander

2½ tsp ground turmeric

1 tsp palm sugar or caster sugar

2-3 red chillies, roughly chopped

juice of 1 lime

salt and black pepper

750g (1lb 10oz) minced chicken

15-18 slider buns

FOR THE SLAW

¼ red cabbage, shredded

1 apple, cut into matchsticks

1 banana shallot, finely sliced

1 large carrot, cut into fine strips

3 tbsp finely chopped coriander

2 tbsp finely chopped mint

1½ tbsp sugar

3 tbsp each rice vinegar and mirin

juice of 1 lime

FOR THE SATAY SAUCE

2 red chillies

1 garlic clove, peeled

1 tbsp finely chopped shallot

½ lemongrass stalk

2cm (¾in) piece of galangal

1 tsp ground coriander

2 tbsp vegetable oil

3 tbsp dark soy sauce

1 tsp sugar

1 tbsp tamarind pulp

200g (7oz) dry-roasted peanuts

1 Prepare the marinade the day before serving the sliders. Add all the slider ingredients except the chicken and buns to a food processor and whizz until smooth, adding a splash more oil or water if needed. Mix with the chicken and form into small patties, each weighing 40-50g (1½-1¾oz). Chill in the fridge, overnight if possible.

2 To make the slaw, mix all the ingredients in a bowl and leave covered in the fridge until needed.

3 To make the satay sauce, place the chillies, garlic, shallot, lemongrass, galangal, coriander, and 150ml (5fl oz) water in a food processor or blender, and whizz until smooth. Heat the oil in a pan and fry the mixture over a medium heat for 10-15 minutes, stirring continuously. Add a splash of water, if needed, to prevent it sticking.

4 Add the soy sauce, sugar, tamarind, and peanuts, and cook over a low heat for a further 5 minutes. Allow to cool, then process the sauce again to break up the peanuts, but without letting it become completely smooth.

5 When ready to serve, heat some vegetable oil in a frying pan and fry the chicken burgers in batches until golden and cooked through.

6 To serve, place a burger in a slider bun, spoon over a dollop of the satay sauce, top with a little slaw, and the bun lid. Serve 3 burgers per person with the remaining slaw on the side in individual bowls.

MAKE IT *extraordinary*

Fresh lemongrass is blended into the marinade to give the patties a fragrant taste.

Similar to ginger but not as hot, galangal has a spicy taste. Use ginger if galangal is unavailable.

Adding peanuts gives the unconventional sliders an authentic satay flavour.

PREP 20 MINUTES, PLUS CHILLING
COOK 45 MINUTES
SERVES 5-6

NASI GORENG WITH SAMBAL BELACAN

Nasi goreng literally means "fried rice" in Indonesian. This version of the recipe features a freshly made sambal belacan chilli paste and satay chicken skewers.

MAKE IT
extraordinary

Unlike a typical Thai satay (see p75), this Indonesian satay marinade is peanut-free.

150g (5½oz) raw king prawns, peeled and deveined (see p244)

60g (2oz) green beans, cut into bite-sized pieces

400g (14oz) cooked white rice

2 tbsp soy sauce, plus extra to serve

1 tsp tamarind concentrate

½ tsp sugar

salt and freshly ground black pepper

4 eggs

prawn crackers, to serve

coriander leaves, to garnish

FOR THE CHICKEN SATAY

2 tbsp coconut milk

1 tsp ground turmeric

½ tsp ground cumin

1 tsp salt

1 tsp sugar

300g (10oz) boneless chicken thighs, cut into bite-sized pieces

1 tsp vegetable oil, for brushing

FOR THE SAMBAL BELACAN

2 finger-length red chillies, roughly chopped

4 garlic cloves

3 round shallots, peeled

½ tsp shrimp paste

4 tbsp vegetable oil

1 Mix the satay marinade ingredients in a bowl. Add the chicken pieces, cover with cling film, and leave in the fridge for at least 4 hours, or overnight. Submerge 10–15 bamboo skewers in water and leave to soak overnight.

2 Remove the chicken from the fridge 20 minutes before cooking and divide between the skewers. Preheat the oven to 150°C (300°F/Gas 2). Brush the chicken with the vegetable oil and fry in a frying pan for 3–4 minutes each side, until cooked through. Keep warm in the oven.

3 Blend the sambal ingredients in a food processor with 1 tbsp of the vegetable oil until smooth. Heat 2 tbsp vegetable oil in a frying pan and fry the paste for about 5 minutes, until it is fragrant and the oil separates from the mixture. Add more oil if the paste is sticking.

Sambal belacan, made with fresh chilli and shrimp paste, gives the nasi goreng plenty of heat.

4 Add the prawns and green beans. Mix well with the sambal. When the prawns turn pink, add the rice, soy sauce, tamarind, and sugar. Continue to fry for another 5 minutes. Season to taste with salt and pepper.

5 While the rice mixture is cooking, heat 1 tbsp of oil in a large non-stick frying pan over a medium heat, and fry the eggs sunny-side up.

6 Serve the rice with the prawn crackers and chicken skewers, topped with a fried egg and garnished with chopped coriander.

PREP 10 MINUTES, PLUS MARINATING
COOK 35 MINUTES
SERVES 4

SPANISH-STYLE COQ AU VIN

Put an Iberian spin on the classic French chicken dish: Rioja wine, stuffed piquillo peppers, black olives, and plenty of chorizo all combine to give this recipe a decidedly Spanish flavour.

Choose a good-quality, spicy chorizo to give the dish plenty of heat from the paprika.

Black olives add a salty note to the Rioja sauce.

2 tbsp plain flour

salt and freshly ground black pepper

4 large chicken thighs

60g (2oz) butter

125g (4½oz) spicy chorizo, diced

2 garlic cloves, crushed

1 carrot, cut into cubes

1 celery stick, roughly chopped

4 tbsp Pedro Ximenez sherry, or brandy

750ml (1¼ pints) red Rioja wine

1 bay leaf

4–5 sprigs of thyme

1 tbsp olive oil

450g (1lb) button onions, peeled

1 tsp brown sugar

1 tsp red wine vinegar

100g (3½oz) black olives, pitted

100g (3½oz) cream cheese-stuffed piquillo peppers

crusty baguette, to serve

1 Season the flour with salt and pepper. Coat the chicken thighs with the seasoned flour, reserving any excess. Melt half the butter in a flameproof casserole, add the chicken thighs, and fry gently until golden brown all over.

2 Add the chorizo, garlic, carrot, and celery, and fry until softened. Add the reserved flour and cook for 1–2 minutes. Pour in the sherry or brandy and the wine, stirring to incorporate any sediment from the bottom of the casserole. Add the bay leaf and thyme, bring to the boil, cover, and simmer for 1 hour.

3 Meanwhile, melt the rest of the butter with the olive oil in a frying pan over a medium heat. Add the onions and fry until just brown. Stir in the sugar, vinegar, and 1 tbsp water. Pour the onion mixture into the casserole with the chicken, and simmer for another 30 minutes, or until the the vegetables are tender and the chicken is cooked through. Add the olives and peppers.

4 Transfer the chicken and vegetables to a hot serving dish. Remove the bay leaf and thyme from the casserole and discard. Skim off any excess fat and boil the cooking liquid for 3–5 minutes, until reduced to the consistency of a sauce. Pour over the chicken and serve with fresh, crusty baguette slices.

PREP 20 MINUTES
COOK 1 HOUR 45 MINUTES
SERVES 4

CHARGRILLED CHICKEN SALAD WITH YOGURT CORONATION DRESSING

This take on coronation chicken turns the sauce – usually bright yellow and mayonnaise-based – into a light yogurt dressing to be drizzled over a salad of grilled chicken, chicory, lettuce, and naan croutons.

Red chicory, or radicchio, has a peppery taste that matches the mild heat of the dressing.

Naan bread croutons give an extra crunch and lift the salad's texture.

4 chicken breasts

olive oil

salt

1 lollo rosso lettuce, torn into bite-sized pieces

1 frisée lettuce, torn into bite-sized pieces

1 red chicory, trimmed and leaves torn

handful of coriander leaves

50g (1¾oz) flaked almonds

50g (1¾oz) golden sultanas

FOR THE CROUTONS

1 naan bread, cut into 2cm (¾in) squares

olive oil, to drizzle

FOR THE DRESSING

250g (9oz) yogurt

50g (1¾oz) mayonnaise

juice of 1 lime

2 tbsp apricot jam

2 tbsp mild curry powder

1 tbsp Worcestershire sauce

1 Preheat the oven to 180°C (350°F/Gas 4). To make the croutons, place the naan pieces on a baking tray and drizzle with a little olive oil. Season with salt. Bake for 6–7 minutes, until golden. Remove from the oven and set aside until ready to serve. Leave the oven on for cooking the chicken.

2 Heat a griddle pan until smoking hot. Drizzle the chicken breasts with a little olive oil and season with salt. Fry for 2 minutes on one side, to get char marks, then flip over and cook the other side. After 2 minutes, flip the chicken breasts again, turning them 90 degrees, to get criss-cross char marks. Cook for 2 minutes and repeat for the other side.

3 Transfer the chicken to a baking tray and place in the oven for 3–4 minutes, until completely cooked through. Remove from the oven. Cut into 2cm (¾in) slices and set aside until ready to serve.

4 For the dressing, place all the ingredients in a bowl and whisk to incorporate. Season with salt to taste.

5 Place the croutons, chicken, and salad leaves in a bowl. Mix well, then pour over the yogurt dressing, scatter with coriander, almonds, and sultanas, and serve.

PREP 10 MINUTES
COOK 25 MINUTES
SERVES 4

CHINESE FIVE-SPICED DUCK IN AN ORANGE SAUCE

East meets West in this recipe, which is inspired by two classic dishes: Chinese roast duck and French duck à l'orange. The duck is coated in a five-spice dry rub and served with an orange, soy, and rice wine sauce.

1 wild duck, about 1kg (2¼lb)

1 tbsp Chinese five-spice powder

FOR THE SAUCE

60g (2oz) light soft brown sugar

3 tbsp rice wine vinegar

3 tbsp soy sauce

2 star anise

2.5cm (1in) piece of fresh root ginger, peeled

1 cinnamon stick

juice of 3 Seville oranges

juice of 2 limes

1-2 tbsp cornflour

1 Preheat the oven to 200°C (400°F/Gas 6). Prick the skin of the duck with a fork and rub all over with the five-spice powder. Place breast-side down on a rack in a roasting tin, and roast in the oven for 30 minutes. Turn the duck over and roast for a further 30 minutes. Remove from the oven, then set aside in a warm place to rest.

2 Meanwhile, peel the oranges (see p242) and cut the peel into fine strips. Blanch in boiling water for 5 minutes, then drain and reserve the zest.

3 Combine the sugar, rice wine vinegar, soy sauce, star anise, ginger, cinnamon stick, orange juice, and lime juice in a saucepan. Stir the mixture and bring it up to a simmer. Mix the cornflour in a cup with 1 tablespoon of water. Stir into the sauce. Simmer briefly until thick and glossy. Add the strips of orange zest. Pour the sauce into a jug.

4 Garnish the roast duck with finely sliced spring onion and red chilli, then serve with the sauce alongside.

MAKE IT *extraordinary*

Chinese five-spice has a mellow heat and an aniseed taste. It works well with fatty meats like duck.

Cinnamon lends a sweet warmth to the sauce, and complements the cinnamon in the five-spice rub.

Bitter-tasting Seville oranges are typically used to make the sauce for duck à l'orange.

PREP 15 MINUTES
COOK 1 HOUR
SERVES 4

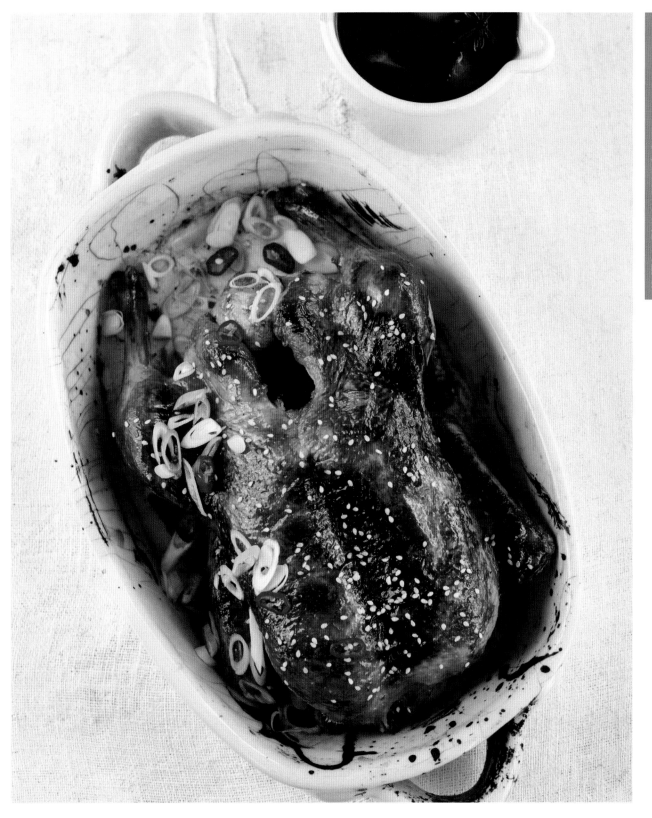

JANE DEVONSHIRE
Champion 2016

Hi I'm Jane Devonshire and I won *MasterChef* in 2016. Following my time on the the show I have written my first cookbook and presented at food festivals all across the country.

Q What's your favourite moment from your time on the show?

A Cooking with Daniel Humm. He made me cook a simple dish of milk and honey for a dessert, and because of that I decided my food wasn't too simple, and I was going to stick to my guns and do what I wanted in those final three dishes. I found him incredibly inspirational.

Q What was your worst kitchen moment?

A During knockout week, for some reason, I could not cook an egg. Conversely, I think it did me a lot of good because it made me up my game and re-evaluate what I was going to do.

Q What was the first recipe you really made your own?

A The one that made people stop and take notice was the lobster and popcorn dish. I knew I had to do something to elevate my food, and it was an idea I had been playing with for a long time.

Q Who is your biggest food hero and why?

A My mum. She taught me to love food, she taught me that the kitchen was a happy place, and she's a brilliant cook.

Q What's your favourite ingredient or kitchen tool?

A Ingredients change throughout the year, but my favourite kitchen tool is without doubt a decent knife. I love gadgets that make my life easier, but you just can't be in the kitchen without a good knife.

Q Best meal of the day: breakfast, lunch, or dinner?

A It has to be one of those lovely long lunches where you just take your time, and it spreads almost into early evening. They are few and far between, but that is just my favourite way of eating.

Q Any advice for potential MasterChefs?

A Be yourself. Don't suddenly decide to start cooking Thai if you've never cooked it before in the kitchen. But most importantly, once I found out I was going on the show, I prepared. I practised every sauce I could think of, taught myself how to fillet any fish, take down any bird, and butcher things. The children tested me, so when I got in the kitchen, I could focus on my combination of flavours. Those staples put me in good stead and helped my confidence as well.

ROAST PHEASANT WITH A CHESTNUT AND CIDER CREAM SAUCE

The rich flavour of roast pheasant pairs beautifully with a black pudding and bacon stuffing, served alongside the autumnal flavours of a chestnut and apple cider sauce.

MAKE IT
extraordinary

Crumble good-quality black pudding into the stuffing to give it a deep, meaty flavour.

Vacuum-packed chestnuts add a sweet, earthy note to the sauce.

2 plump hen pheasants
6 smoked streaky bacon rashers
50g (1¾oz) unsalted butter
salt and freshly ground black pepper

FOR THE STUFFING
75g (2½oz) unsalted butter
6 smoked streaky bacon rashers, finely chopped
2 banana shallots, finely chopped
3–4 sprigs thyme, leaves picked
2 garlic cloves, finely chopped or grated
100g (3½oz) fatty black pudding, crumbled or finely chopped
150g (5½oz) panko breadcrumbs

FOR THE SAUCE
1 shallot, finely chopped
3–4 sprigs of thyme
25g (scant 1oz) unsalted butter
180g packet of vacuum-packed chestnuts, chopped
250ml (8fl oz) chicken stock
250ml (8fl oz) dry cider
125ml (4fl oz) double cream

1 Preheat the oven to 200°C (400°F/Gas 6). To make the stuffing, melt the butter in a large frying pan, and when foaming add the bacon, shallots, thyme, garlic, and black pudding. Fry over a low heat for 5–6 minutes, until the shallot is cooked but not coloured. Remove from the heat and mix in the breadcrumbs. Season with black pepper. Leave to cool.

2 Untruss the pheasants and use a spoon to fill the cavity with the stuffing, pushing it in firmly. Smear liberally with the butter and season with salt and pepper, then drape the bacon over the birds, making sure the legs are covered. Place in the preheated oven and cook for 30 minutes.

3 Meanwhile, make the sauce. Gently fry the shallot and thyme in the butter for about 5 minutes, until transparent. Add the chopped chestnuts and chicken stock and simmer until about two-thirds of the stock has evaporated. Add the cider, bring to the boil, and then simmer until two-thirds of the liquid has evaporated. Remove from the heat, stir in the cream, and season to taste.

4 Remove the birds from the oven and lift off the bacon. If it's not crispy, place it in the pan next to the pheasants. Baste the birds and roast for another 15–20 minutes, until pink and juicy when pierced with a knife just above the leg joint. Remove from the oven and leave to rest for 10 minutes.

5 To serve, place one leg and one breast on each plate with a good spoonful of the stuffing, a slice of the crispy bacon, and the sauce poured on the side.

PREP TIME 10 MINUTES, PLUS COOLING
COOK TIME 1 HOUR
SERVES 4

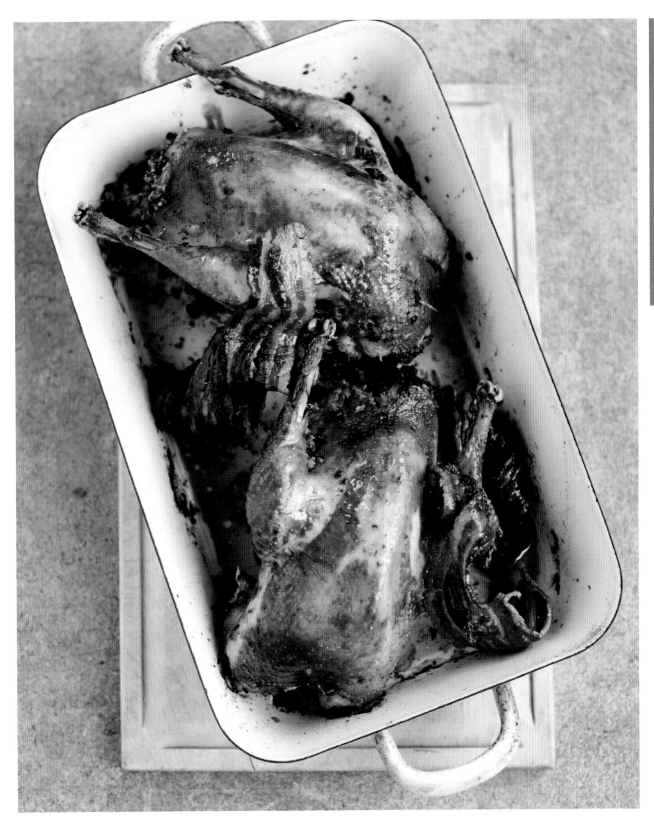

SPICED CHRISTMAS TURKEY

No Christmas is complete without turkey, and this richly spiced turkey, with matching confit and stuffing, is unlike any other. Serve with all the trimmings (see pp172-77).

4kg (9lb) turkey leg and crown, separated

2 litres (3½ pints) chicken stock

50g (1¾oz) butter, plus extra for frying

salt and black pepper

100ml (3½fl oz) ghee or clarified butter, at room temperature

1 tsp each garam masala, ground cumin, and ginger

½ tsp turmeric

FOR THE SPICED BRINE

1 orange, cut into quarters

200g (7oz) sugar

120ml (4fl oz) honey

2 onions, cut into quarters

250g (9oz) sea salt

1 cinnamon stick

2 tbsp each allspice berries and white mustard seeds

1 tbsp coriander seeds

1 tsp cumin seeds

4 each cloves and star anise

FOR THE STUFFING

50g (1¾oz) butter, plus extra for greasing

1 onion, finely chopped

450g (1lb) sausage meat

125g (4½oz) white breadcrumbs

1 egg

1 apple, finely chopped

2 tsp garam masala

1 tsp each ground coriander, cumin, and paprika

½ tsp turmeric

1 tbsp mango chutney

2 garlic cloves, finely grated

1 tsp finely chopped thyme

1 Make the brine. Squeeze the orange pieces over a large pan filled with 6 litres (10 pints) of water. Add the remaining brine ingredients, then whisk to dissolve the sugar and salt. Submerge the turkey crown, adding more water if required. Marinate for 1 day.

2 Preheat the oven to 130°C (250°F/Gas ½). Add the turkey legs to a roasting dish. Cover with stock and braise for 5-7 hours, until the meat is soft. Allow to cool. Pass the stock through a sieve and set aside. Pick the meat from the legs, discarding the skin. Skim the fat from the stock and mix into the meat with the butter, then season. Place three 1m (3ft) layers of cling film onto a work surface. Spread the meat along one short edge, then roll up the film to form a ballotine, twisting the ends to secure. Refrigerate until ready to serve, then remove from the film, slice, and fry in a little butter.

3 Remove the turkey crown 1-2 hours before cooking and dry very well. Preheat the oven to 200°C (400°F/Gas 6). Combine the ghee and spices to form a paste, then rub half the paste between the breast and skin, and the remaining paste over the skin. Put the crown in a large, deep roasting tin and season inside and out. Roast for 20 minutes, then reduce the temperature to 190°C (375°F/Gas 5), cover loosely with foil, and roast for 20 minutes per 450g (1lb), plus 20 minutes, basting hourly. Remove the foil for the last 10-15 minutes. Pierce the bird with a skewer: it is cooked when the juices run clear. Leave to rest in a warm place, uncovered, for 15 minutes.

4 Meanwhile, for the stuffing, melt the butter in a pan over a medium heat. Sweat the onion until soft but not coloured, and allow to cool. Add the remaining ingredients, mix well, and press into a greased baking dish. Cook for 30-40 minutes at 190°C (375°F/Gas 5) until piping hot. Allow to rest before serving with the turkey crown and fried ballotine confit slices.

MAKE IT
extraordinary

Spread the homemade spice paste over the turkey crown skin to flavour the meat.

Prepare the spiced turkey leg confit ahead of time, then fry it just before serving the crown.

PREP 1 HOUR 30 MINUTES, PLUS MARINATING
COOK 10 HOURS
SERVES 8

XIAN-STYLE ROAST LEG OF LAMB WITH SHAOXING GRAVY

With a spice rub inspired by Xian spices and a gravy enriched with Shaoxing rice wine, this Chinese take on roast lamb is full of flavour.

2kg (4½lb) leg of lamb
600ml (1 pint) hot lamb or beef stock
1 tsp redcurrant jelly
splash of Shaoxing wine
salt and freshly ground black pepper
broccoli and pak choi, to serve

FOR THE SPICE RUB
2 tbsp crushed dried chillies
1 tbsp cumin seeds
1 tbsp fennel seeds
1 tsp salt
1 tsp dried garlic flakes

1 Preheat the oven to 200°C (400°F/Gas 6). To make the spice rub, toast the crushed dried chillies, cumin seeds, and fennel seeds in a dry frying pan, then grind them to a coarse powder in a pestle and mortar. Mix in the salt and garlic flakes.

2 Pierce the skin of the lamb all over with the point of a sharp knife. Rub the spice mixture into the skin.

3 Place the lamb in a large roasting tin and cook in the oven for about 15 minutes, until it begins to brown. Reduce the oven temperature to 180°C (350°F/Gas 4) and continue to roast for a further 1 hour (for rare) to 1½ hours (for well done), basting with the juices halfway through the cooking time. Transfer the lamb to a large plate, cover with foil, and leave to rest in a warm place.

4 While the lamb is resting, make the gravy. Wearing an oven mitt, hold the roasting tin at a slight angle over a high heat on the hob. Add the stock, redcurrant jelly, and Shaoxing wine, and bring to the boil, scraping up any bits from the bottom of the tin with a wooden spoon. Reduce the heat slightly and simmer, stirring continuously, for 5-8 minutes. Season to taste.

5 Carve the lamb at the table, and serve with broccoli, pak choi, and the gravy in a jug alongside.

MAKE IT
extraordinary

A combination of chilli, cumin, and fennel form the basis of the lamb's Xian-style spice rub.

Use Shaoxing wine to deglaze the roasting tin and turn the spicy lamb juices into a gravy.

PREP 15 MINUTES
COOK 1 HOUR 55 MINUTES, PLUS RESTING
SERVES 6-8

LAMB CUTLETS WITH POMEGRANATE AND LABNEH

Instead of the traditional British pairing of lamb and rosemary, these lamb cutlets are glazed with a rich pomegranate molasses marinade and served with bulgur wheat and homemade labneh – a thick and creamy Middle Eastern cheese.

Pomegranate molasses, an intensely fruity, sweet-sour syrup, is used to glaze the lamb.

A mix of thyme, sesame, and sumac, za'atar adds a citrussy, woody flavour to the labneh.

8–10 lamb cutlets
1½ tbsp olive oil
2 tbsp chopped coriander leaves
2 tbsp chopped mint leaves
2 tsp ground cumin
1 tsp ground coriander
3 tbsp pomegranate molasses
salt and freshly ground black pepper

FOR THE LABNEH
450ml (15fl oz) extra thick full-fat Greek-style yogurt
1 tsp sea salt
2 tbsp za'atar
2 tbsp extra virgin olive oil

FOR THE BULGUR WHEAT
200g (7oz) bulgur wheat
175g (6oz) frozen broad beans (shelled)
6 tbsp olive oil
1 garlic clove, crushed
handful of chopped parsley and chopped mint leaves

TO GARNISH
coriander leaves
pomegranate seeds
squeeze of lemon juice

1 To make the labneh, line a bowl with muslin and pour in the yogurt. Stir in the salt, then bring the edges of the muslin together to form a bundle, and tie it up with string. Hang the bundle over the kitchen sink for around 4 hours, to let liquid drain off. Transfer to a bowl and mix in the za'atar and olive oil.

2 Preheat the oven to 200°C (400°F/Gas 6). In a bowl, mix together the olive oil, herbs, spices, and the pomegranate molasses. Season with salt and pepper. Add the lamb, coat thoroughly in the mixture, and leave to marinate for 15 minutes at room temperature.

3 Roast the lamb for 10 minutes (rare), 15 minutes (medium), or 20 minutes (well done). Leave to rest, loosely covered with foil, for 5 minutes.

4 Meanwhile, cook the bulgur wheat in boiling salted water for 12 minutes, then add the broad beans and cook for a further 3 minutes. Drain well, then leave to cool slightly before tossing together with the oil, garlic, and herbs.

5 Serve 2–3 cutlets per portion, accompanied by the bulgur wheat and a generous spoonful of the labneh. Garnish with coriander leaves, pomegranate seeds, and a squeeze of lemon juice.

PREP 10 MINUTES, PLUS DRAINING
COOK 25 MINUTES
SERVES 4

IRISH SWEETBREAD STEW

Featuring a lamb breast ballotine, slow-cooked lamb neck, and pan-fried sweetbreads, this sophisticated take on Irish stew is as flavourful as it is elegant.

MAKE IT
extraordinary

Fry sweetbreads in rosemary and garlic for a tasty addition to the other lamb cuts on the plate.

FOR THE BALLOTINE

2 lamb breasts

1 tbsp vegetable oil

1 leek, roughly chopped

1 carrot, roughly chopped

1 onion, roughly chopped

1 celery stick, roughly chopped

1.5 litres (2¾ pints) vegetable stock

5 peppercorns

1 bay leaf

salt and freshly ground black pepper

FOR THE STEW

1 lamb whole neck fillet

4 sprigs of thyme

130g (4³/₄oz) pearl barley

8 baby onions, peeled

12 baby carrots

200g (7oz) swede, cut into 2cm (¾in) cubes

4 potatoes, cut into 2cm (¾in) cubes

75g (2½oz) butter

8 lamb sweetbreads, pre-soaked (see p245)

2 tbsp flour

1 garlic clove

1 sprig of rosemary

1 Preheat the oven to 130°C (250°F/Gas ½). In a flameproof casserole, brown the lamb breasts all over, then remove. Add the oil and vegetables and fry for 4–5 minutes, until they start to brown, then add the stock, peppercorns, and bay leaf. Return the lamb to the dish, ensuring it is just covered with stock. Cover and braise in the oven for 7–9 hours, until the meat is flaking and tender. Allow to cool for about 1 hour, then remove the meat and strain the liquid though a fine sieve, retaining the liquid and discarding the vegetables. Flake the meat, discarding any sinew and skin. Skim the fat from the cooking liquid, stir into the meat, and season. Roll the meat into a ballotine (see p88, step 2). Refrigerate to set.

2 Place the cooking liquid in a pan, and boil to reduce it to about 1 litre (1¾ pints). Sear the neck fillet in a heavy flameproof casserole until browned all over. Add the thyme and reduced liquid, place over a high heat, and bring to the boil, skimming off any scum. Cover and simmer gently for 3 hours, stirring occasionally, then remove from the heat and allow to cool slightly. Remove the neck fillet and keep warm. Strain the liquid into a pan. Add the barley and baby onions to the liquid and simmer for about 30 minutes, until the barley is cooked.

3 Blanch the baby carrots, swede, and potatoes in boiling salted water until tender, then toss with a knob of butter and season to taste. Blanch the sweetbreads in salted boiling water for 30 seconds, then plunge into iced water. Remove the membranes and sinew. Pat dry, then dust with seasoned flour and fry with the remaining butter, garlic, and rosemary over a medium heat for about 4 minutes each side. Remove and keep warm. Carve the neck fillet into 4 portions. Divide the ballotine into 8 slices and fry in a little oil for about 2 minutes each side, until coloured. To serve, arrange the ballotine, neck fillet, sweetbreads, and vegetables on plates, and garnish with the onions, barley, and the sauce from the barley pan.

PREP 1 HOUR 30 MINUTES
COOK 13 HOURS 30 MINUTES, PLUS COOLING
SERVES 4

MOROCCAN LAMB TAGINE WITH SAFFRON AND RAS EL HANOUT

This tagine is made extra special with the addition of ras el hanout spices, along with saffron, which is ground with water in a pestle and mortar to extract as much of the threads' flavour as possible. It is traditionally eaten off one platter as a celebratory meal, especially at weddings.

Ras el hanout is a North African spice mix that gives the tagine a pungent, aromatic flavour.

1 large onion, thinly sliced

5 tbsp olive oil, plus extra for the almonds and sesame seeds

2 garlic cloves, finely chopped

bunch of coriander and parsley tied into a bouquet using butcher's cooking string, plus extra parsley to garnish

500g (1lb 2oz) lamb shanks

6 saffron threads

1 tsp ras el hanout

1 tsp ground cumin

1 tsp ground turmeric

1 tsp ground ginger

salt and freshly ground black pepper

175g (6oz) pitted prunes

75g (2½oz) whole blanched almonds

3 tbsp sesame seeds

cooked couscous, to serve

1 In a tagine, sweat the onion in the oil for 5–7 minutes, until it begins to caramelize. Add the garlic and the coriander and parsley bouquet, followed by the lamb shanks, and cook until the meat is evenly browned.

2 In a pestle and mortar, grind the saffron threads with a few teaspoons of water to make a bright yellow liquid. Add a little more water, then pour into a jug and add enough water to make up to 475ml (16fl oz), then add to the lamb. Add the spices, cover, and cook over a medium heat for 1½ hours.

3 The tagine should be sticky and the sauce reduced. Add more water if necessary, then season to taste with salt and pepper. Add the prunes and continue to cook for 10 minutes.

4 Meanwhile, fry the almonds in a little oil until they are browned on all sides, then set aside. Repeat with the sesame seeds, frying them for just a few seconds, as they burn very quickly.

5 To serve, spoon the couscous onto a big platter and place the lamb shanks on top. Scatter over the almonds, sesame seeds, and a sprinkling of fresh parsley.

Use a pestle and mortar to maximize the flavour released by the saffron threads.

PREP 10 MINUTES
COOK 2 HOURS
SERVES 4

NATALIE COLEMAN
Champion 2013

My name is Natalie Coleman and I won *MasterChef* in 2013. I've since gone on to set up and become an ambassador for a children's cookery school in London, and I've also written for several cookbooks.

Q What's your favourite moment from your time on the show?

A My favourite moment from the show was when Marcus Wareing came in to judge the invention test. He said I had created "perfection on the plate". I was very happy about that.

Q What was the first recipe you really made your own?

A The recipe that I feel I have owned since the show is the Scotch egg. I make all sorts of variations of them, and they go down a treat with customers.

Q Who is your biggest food hero and why?

A Either Tom Kerridge or Daniel Clifford. I did stages with both of them and they are legends. Their food is out of this world.

Q What's your favourite ingredient or kitchen tool?

A My favourite ingredient is thyme, because it makes everything taste great, and you can even use it in desserts. My best tool has to be a kitchen blender, because it makes purées very smooth.

Q What was your worst kitchen moment?

A One of my worst kitchen moments was when I was practising one of my dishes for *MasterChef* and I nearly chopped off my thumb. My grandad and I sat in A&E for four hours on a Saturday night, and then I had to continue the competition while it was bandaged up and very sore.

Q Best meal of the day: breakfast, lunch, or dinner?

A My favourite meal has got to be dinner. I don't like breakfast because I'm always in a rush. I prefer dinner because you can just sit down, eat loads, and go into a food coma afterwards.

Q Any advice for potential MasterChefs?

A Be persistent and practise loads. It took me five years to get on the show. Just stick with it and be true to yourself.

CHILLI CON CARNE SAMOSAS

Serve up a rich, slow-cooked Mexican chilli con carne in deep-fried filo pastry as crisp, samosa-style parcels, with plenty of fresh salsa and guacamole alongside.

MAKE IT
extraordinary

Fold each strip of filo over itself several times to form triangular, multi-layered parcels.

Add a cinnamon stick to infuse the chilli with a gentle warmth.

400g (14oz) lean beef mince

2 tbsp olive oil

1 onion, finely diced

1 red pepper, diced

1 tbsp tomato purée

1 cinnamon stick

½ tsp each cayenne pepper, chilli powder, garlic powder, ground coriander, and ground cumin

1 tbsp smoked paprika

2 star anise

400g can chopped tomatoes

150ml (5fl oz) beef stock

2 tbsp Worcestershire sauce

½ tsp sugar

400g can kidney beans, drained and rinsed

salt and freshly ground black pepper

1 packet of filo pastry sheets

2 litres of oil, for deep-fat frying

50g (1¾oz) melted butter

fresh guacamole (see p42), to serve

FOR THE SALSA

200g (7oz) cherry tomatoes, cut into quarters

2 tbsp finely chopped coriander leaves

½ red onion, finely chopped

juice and zest of 1 lime

1 tsp crushed dried chillies

a few drops of Tabasco sauce

1 Heat a large frying pan over a medium heat and cook the beef in 1 tbsp of olive oil until browned all over. Remove from the heat and sieve to drain the fat. Set aside.

2 In a large pan, sweat the onion in the remaining olive oil until softened. Add the red pepper and cook for 3–4 minutes, until it starts to soften. Add the tomato purée and spices and cook for another 1–2 minutes, stirring to combine. Add the beef and cook for another 2–3 minutes.

3 Add the chopped tomatoes, beef stock, Worcestershire sauce, and sugar, and bring to the boil, then reduce to a simmer. Add the kidney beans and cook for 1½ hours, until the sauce is thick. Season to taste, remove the cinnamon stick and star anise, and leave to cool to room temperature.

4 To make the salsa, mix all the ingredients in a bowl and season with salt and Tabasco to taste. Set aside until ready to serve.

5 To make the samosas, cut a sheet of filo pastry lengthways into long strips about 7.5cm (3in) wide. Brush a strip with melted butter, then place 2 tbsp of the chilli filling in one corner. Fold over in a triangle shape, then fold again until all the pastry strip has been used. Brush the last fold and the finished samosa with melted butter. Repeat with the remaining pastry and filling.

6 Preheat a deep-fat fryer to 180°C (350°F) and fry the samosas in batches for 3–5 minutes, until golden brown. Drain on kitchen paper, season with salt, and serve with the salsa and fresh guacamole.

Serve the samosas with a homemade salsa, boosted with a few drops of Tabasco sauce.

PREP 25 MINUTES
COOK 2 HOURS
SERVES 4

ROAST BEEF DIP WITH BONE MARROW

Turn the leftovers of a classic roast beef dinner into an American-style "beef dip" sandwich with freshly made horseradish mayonnaise and roasted bone marrow.

MAKE IT
extraordinary

Most butchers will be able to supply you with fresh bones to serve alongside the beef dip.

3.5kg (7lb) bone-in rib of beef
3 carrots, roughly chopped
3 celery sticks, roughly chopped
2 onions, roughly chopped
1 garlic bulb, sliced in half
4 bay leaves
350ml (12fl oz) red wine
1 litre (1¾ pints) beef stock
2 tbsp cornflour
1 tbsp redcurrant jelly
6 beef bones with marrow in
salt and black pepper
100g (3½oz) watercress
juice of ½ lemon
6 warm baguette rolls

FOR THE MARINADE

1 tbsp black peppercorns
3 sprigs rosemary, leaves only
10 sprigs thyme, leaves only
3 garlic cloves, grated
4 tbsp English mustard
6 tbsp rapeseed oil, plus extra
   for drizzling
2 tbsp Maldon salt

FOR THE PARSLEY OIL

250g (9oz) parsley
150ml (5½fl oz) groundnut oil

FOR THE MAYONNAISE

250ml (9fl oz) rapeseed oil
2 egg yolks
½ tsp mustard powder
1 tsp white wine vinegar
1 tbsp horseradish sauce

1 Prepare the marinade. Grind the peppercorns in a pestle and mortar, add the remaining marinade ingredients, and grind to make a smooth paste. Score the beef fat with a sharp knife in a crisscross pattern, rub in the paste, and chill overnight.

2 Allow the beef to reach room temperature. Preheat the oven to 200°C (400°F/Gas 6). Place the vegetables, garlic bulb, and bay leaves in a roasting tray, drizzle with a little oil and place in the oven for 5 minutes. Remove from the oven and set the beef on top. Cook for 1¾ hours (medium rare) to 2¼ hours (well done). Remove the beef from the oven, wrap in foil, and rest for 25 minutes. Reserve the vegetables and cooking juices.

3 Add the red wine, stock, and the vegetables and cooking juices to a saucepan. Bring to the boil, then simmer for 20 minutes. Strain the juices through a fine sieve, discarding the vegetables, then return to the pan and continue cooking until reduced by a third. Mix the cornflour with 4 tbsp cold water and add to the saucepan with the jelly, whisking for 1-2 minutes, until thickened. Set aside.

4 Make the parsley oil (see p250). Set aside until ready to serve. Prepare the mayonnaise (see p246), incorporating the horseradish and the vinegar. Add 1-2 tsp water if the mayonnaise seems too thick. Set aside until ready to serve.

5 For the roasted bone marrow, preheat the oven to 200°C (400°F/Gas 6). Place the bones in a baking tray, season, and cook for 20 minutes until bubbling. To serve, dress the watercress with some of the parsley oil, lemon juice, and salt. Slice the beef thinly. Spread mayonnaise on the split baguettes, fill with a generous helping of the beef and watercress, and serve with the dip and a piece of bone marrow.

PREP 35 MINUTES, PLUS MARINATING
COOK 3 HOURS
SERVES 6

CARAMELIZED RIBEYE BEEF TERIYAKI WITH CRISPY GARLIC CHIPS

Instead of a simple beef teriyaki stir-fry, why not opt for a seriously indulgent cut of meat to serve with this classic Japanese sauce? A juicy cut of ribeye steak paired with roasted shallots and crisp garlic chips makes for a hearty, flavourful meal in this recipe.

MAKE IT *extraordinary*

Shallow-fry thin slices of garlic to make crisp chips, and use them to garnish the sticky ribeye teriyaki.

100ml (3½fl oz) soy sauce
100ml (3½fl oz) mirin
3 tbsp sake
50g (1¾oz) dark brown sugar
2 garlic cloves, crushed (optional)
2cm (½in) fresh root ginger, thinly sliced
4 ribeye steaks
5-6 banana shallots
2 tbsp vegetable oil
salt
1-2 tsp cornflour

FOR THE GARLIC CHIPS
4 garlic cloves, thinly sliced
vegetable oil, for frying

1 Preheat the oven to 180°C (350°F/Gas 4). Combine the soy sauce, mirin, sake, sugar, garlic, and ginger in a small pan. Bring to a boil, then simmer until it is reduced by one-quarter. Allow to cool, then remove the garlic and ginger. Place the steaks in a shallow dish and pour over the marinade. Cover and set aside for about 30 minutes at room temperature.

2 Meanwhile, peel and halve the banana shallots. Place them in a roasting tin with the vegetable oil and a pinch of salt and toss to coat. Roast for about 45 minutes, until the shallots are very soft and caramelized.

3 Make the garlic chips. Place the garlic slices in a frying pan filled to a depth of about 1cm (½in) with vegetable oil. Set over a medium-low heat for at least 10 minutes, letting the garlic gently brown. When golden, remove with a slotted spoon, drain on kitchen paper and set aside.

4 Remove the steaks from the marinade and set aside. Pour the remaining marinade into a small pan and bring to the boil over a high heat. Mix the cornflour with 2-3 tsp of cold water and stir into the sauce to thicken it. Simmer for 10 minutes.

5 Preheat the grill on its highest setting, and line a grill tray with foil. Grill the steaks for 2-3 minutes on each side, until medium-rare, or for longer if you prefer. Pour over the marinade sauce and finish the steaks with a blowtorch to caramelize the marinade. Serve with the roasted shallots and crispy garlic chips.

PREP 10 MINUTES, PLUS MARINATING
COOK 45 MINUTES
SERVES 4

MALAYSIAN STREET BURGER

Far more than a simple hamburger, this recipe is inspired by a Malaysian street food staple, with a double layer of marinaded patties wrapped in a thin omelette.

300g (10oz) minced beef
200g (7oz) minced pork
1 large knob of butter
4 eggs
4 slices of cheese
4 burger buns, toasted
2 beef tomatoes, sliced
4–8 iceberg lettuce leaves
120ml (4fl oz) mayonnaise
90ml (3fl oz) sweet chilli sauce

FOR THE MARINADE
2 tsp onion granules
2 tsp garlic granules
2 tsp light soy sauce
2 tsp Malaysian curry powder
   or madras curry powder
2 tsp cornflour
1 tsp salt
1/2 tsp sugar
1/4 tsp ground white pepper

1 Place the beef, pork, and the marinade ingredients in a large bowl. Mix well and chill for at least 1 hour in the fridge. Divide into 8 evenly sized balls and flatten with your palm to a thickness of 1cm (1/2in). If you are not cooking them immediately, keep the patties refrigerated, but remove them from the fridge at least 30 minutes before cooking.

2 Preheat the oven to 100°C (200°F/Gas 1/4). Melt the butter in a frying pan and cook the patties in batches. They need about 1 minute each side (longer for well done). Transfer to a baking tray lined with baking parchment and keep warm in the oven. Repeat until all are cooked. Pour off some of the fat into a small pot then return the pan to the heat.

3 Remove 4 patties from the oven. Lightly beat 1 egg, pour into the pan, and spread out thinly, like you would do a pancake. When it starts to cook through, place one of the patties on top and wrap the egg around it. Remove and set aside. Repeat with 3 further patties, frying them in the reserved fat. Return the 4 egg-wrapped patties to the oven to keep warm.

4 For the remaining 4 patties, place a slice of cheese on top of each, and place under the grill until melted. Halve the burger buns and lightly toast them under the grill.

5 To assemble, spread mayonnaise generously onto both sides of a bun. To the bottom half, add lettuce, then the egg-wrapped patty, another layer of mayonnaise, and a dollop of sweet chilli sauce, followed by the cheese-topped patty. Add tomato and more lettuce, and finally the bun top. Repeat for the remaining burgers and serve.

MAKE IT
extraordinary

Malaysian curry powder contains a unique blend of spices, and is also used to make rendang.

Top the patties with a hot, tangy sweet chilli sauce.

PREP 10 MINUTES, PLUS CHILLING
COOK 30 MINUTES
SERVES 4

DHRUV BAKER
Champion 2010

I'm Dhruv Baker and I won *MasterChef* in 2010. Since the show I've worked in some of the top kitchens in the country, and owned several food and catering companies, including my own pub/restaurant.

Q What's your favourite moment from your time on the show?

A Other than winning, it would have to be cooking in Jodhpur for the Maharaja and his family. A truly once in a lifetime moment, and one I will always remember.

Q What was the first recipe you really made your own?

A During *MasterChef*, it was the duck dish using Indian spices. It was based on a chicken recipe my mother has made for years, and I tweaked and adapted it and made it genuinely my own. It was the first time that Gregg and John really paid attention to my style of cooking.

Q Who is your biggest food hero and why?

A My mother's great-uncle, who wrote a book called *The Cooking Delights of the Indian Maharajas*. Some of the recipes are still relevant today, and they're delicious.

Q What's your favourite ingredient or kitchen tool and why?

A My favourite ingredient and piece of equipment is my spice tin. You can take the most basic recipe and elevate it with these magical ingredients.

Q What was your worst kitchen moment?

A I've had many kitchen-related disasters, but the one that stands out is after I dropped my family off at Gatwick airport. Coming home, I got stuck in traffic for $2\frac{1}{2}$ hours, and when I turned into my road I could see plumes of smoke. I had been slow-cooking something while I was out, but I hadn't planned on the delay, and the pan had burnt through.

Q Best meal of the day: breakfast, lunch, or dinner?

A One of the beauties about being a grown-up is that you can eat ice cream for breakfast, pork chops for breakfast, or cereal for dinner. I think brunch is ideal, because if you get it right you only need to eat once, and then it's all about the long siesta in the afternoon.

Q Any advice for potential MasterChefs?

A Cook the type of food that your friends and family ate when they told you to apply. Don't go onto the show and then change everything you've always done. Cook from the heart, and you'll go further than if you try and cook what you think the judges want to see.

BEEF AND PANCETTA PAPPARDELLE AL RAGÙ WITH TRUFFLE OIL

Slow-cooked shredded beef clings to wide strips of pappardelle pasta in this Italian staple. In this recipe, diced pancetta and star anise are included to give the ragù an additional salty, spicy complexity, while a final drizzle of truffle oil gives the dish a touch of luxury.

Diced pancetta is added early in the cooking process to give the ragù a salty depth.

4 tbsp olive oil

400g (14oz) beef (brisket, shin, or braising), cut into 4-6 pieces

salt and freshly ground black pepper

30g (1oz) butter

100g (3½oz) white mushrooms, sliced

100g (3½oz) pancetta, diced

1 small onion, finely chopped

1 celery stick, finely chopped

1 carrot, finely chopped

4 garlic cloves, skin on

1 star anise

3 fresh bay leaves

250ml (9fl oz) red wine

500ml (16fl oz) beef stock

400g can chopped tomatoes

450g (1lb) dried pappardelle pasta

Parmesan cheese, grated, to serve

drizzle of truffle oil, to serve

1 Preheat the oven to 160°C (325°F/Gas 3). Heat 2 tbsp of olive oil in a heavy, lidded flameproof casserole large enough to fit all the ingredients over a medium heat. Season the beef with salt and cook for 10-15 minutes, until browned on all sides. Remove with a slotted spoon and set aside.

2 Add the butter and the remaining 2 tbsp of olive oil to the casserole, and fry the mushrooms for 5-10 minutes, until starting to turn golden. Add the pancetta and fry for a further 5 minutes. Add the onion, celery, carrot, garlic, star anise, and bay leaves, and continue to fry gently, stirring occasionally, for 10 minutes, until softened but not browned.

3 Return the meat to the casserole, increase the heat, and pour in the wine. Simmer for 10 minutes, until reduced by half, stir in the stock and tomatoes, and bring back to the boil.

4 Place the lid on the casserole and cook in the oven for 3-3½ hours, stirring every 20 minutes or so. If the liquid dries up completely, add a little water. It is done when the meat still holds its shape but is just starting to fall apart.

5 Remove from the oven and lift out the garlic, bay leaves, and star anise. Roughly shred the meat using 2 forks.

6 Meanwhile, cook the pappardelle in boiling, salted water according to the packet instructions, until al dente. Drain well, tip into the beef ragù, stir well, and serve with freshly grated Parmesan and a drizzle of the truffle oil.

Star anise introduces a mild, liquorice-like element to the rich beef ragù.

Drizzle the dish with a little truffle oil before serving to add a final aromatic note.

PREP 10 MINUTES
COOK 4 HOURS 15 MINUTES
SERVES 4

SHREDDED BEEF DAUBE WITH FENNEL

This take on a traditional French daube combines a melt-in-the-mouth shredded beef with larger cuts of stewing steak, while the fennel-enriched red wine marinade forms the basis of a thick, glossy sauce.

700g (1½lb) lean beef steak cut into 3–4cm (1½in) chunks

4 x 200g (7oz) pieces lean stewing beef steak

2 tbsp olive oil

100g (3½oz) lardons or diced pancetta, plus extra to serve

1 tbsp plain flour, seasoned with salt and pepper

500ml (16fl oz) beef stock

25g (scant 1oz) cold butter, cut into cubes

fennel fronds, to garnish

FOR THE MARINADE

2 garlic cloves, crushed

3 banana shallots, chopped

3 bay leaves

2 celery sticks, chopped

1 small fennel bulb, very finely sliced

2 tsp fennel seeds

7cm (3in) strip of dried orange peel

10 black peppercorns

2 sprigs of thyme

2 sprigs of rosemary

2 sprigs of flat-leaf parsley

375ml (13fl oz) red wine

1 In a large bowl, combine the beef chunks with all the marinade ingredients. Stir well to combine, cover, and refrigerate overnight.

2 Remove the beef chunks from the marinade and wipe thoroughly with kitchen paper. Strain the marinade through a sieve into a bowl. Reserve both the ingredients and the liquid.

3 Pour the oil into a large flameproof roasting tin, add the lardons or pancetta, and fry over a medium heat for 2–3 minutes, until sizzling. Coat the 4 large pieces of beef in the flour and fry until brown all over. Add the small pieces of beef and cook for 10 minutes, until brown. Add the reserved marinade ingredients and cook, stirring, for 5 minutes, then pour in the liquid and cook for another 10 minutes to burn off the alcohol. Add the stock and bring to the boil. Reduce the heat to low, cover, and cook for 2½–3 hours, until the beef is very tender. After 2 hours, remove the herbs, and stir.

4 Remove the 4 large pieces of meat, and keep warm. Using a slotted spoon, remove the small pieces and shred them using 2 forks. Reheat the shredded meat with some of the sauce in a small pan. Strain the remaining sauce through a sieve, discard the sieve contents, and bring the sauce to the boil. Simmer, uncovered, for 15 minutes to thicken the sauce. Remove from the heat and whisk in the cold butter until glossy and thick. Place a large piece of beef on each plate, top with shredded beef, pour over the glossy sauce, and garnish with fried lardons and fennel fronds.

MAKE IT
extraordinary

Fresh fennel adds an aniseed note to the daube marinade. Reserve the fronds for garnish.

Full-bodied red wine matches the richness of the beef to create a flavourful marinade and sauce.

PREP 20 MINUTES, PLUS MARINATING
COOK 3 HOURS 40 MINUTES
SERVES 4

SLOW-COOKED HAM AND PEA TERRINE WITH WILD GARLIC

Make the most of a piece of gammon by turning it into a flavourful, salty–sweet terrine. The meat is slow-cooked to make it deliciously flaky, then layered with peas and and wrapped in bright green wild garlic leaves.

MAKE IT
extraordinary

Wild garlic leaves lend their strong fragrance and sweet, delicate taste to the terrine.

1kg (2lb) piece of boned and rolled gammon
2 tbsp Dijon mustard
4 tbsp demerara sugar
2 tbsp runny honey
250ml (9fl oz) white wine
4 tsp gelatine powder
about 20 wild garlic leaves
300g (10oz) frozen peas

1 Carefully place the gammon, skin-side up, into a slow cooker. Mix the mustard, sugar, and honey, and wine and add to the slow cooker with 250ml (9fl oz) water. Set the slow cooker on a low setting, cover, and leave for 6–8 hours.

2 When cooked, remove the ham and reserve the cooking liquor. Carefully remove the skin from the meat and discard, then shred the meat using 2 forks.

3 Place the gelatine in a small bowl and cover with 4 tbsp of cold water.

4 In a saucepan, simmer the cooking liquor over a moderate heat until reduced by two-thirds. Remove from the heat and stir in the gelatine, ensuring it is fully dissolved.

5 Prepare a 1kg (2lb) loaf tin or terrine dish by lining it with several layers of cling film, large enough to cover the top when the tin is filled. Then line the tin with wild garlic leaves, overlapping them along the length of the tin. Reserve enough leaves to to cover the top when the tin is filled.

6 Alternate a 1cm (½in) layer of the warm ham with a layer of peas and a little of the cooking liquor, pressing each layer to remove any air or excess liquor. Finish with a layer of meat slightly proud of the top. Cover with the remaining wild garlic leaves, then the cling film, and place on a tray to catch any excess liquid. Add a weight on top and refrigerate for at least 6 hours before serving.

PREP 30 MINUTES, PLUS CHILLING
COOK 8 HOURS
SERVES 8

STICKY SLOW-COOKED PORK RIBS

To take ribs to the next level, try slow-cooking them. This recipe features two slow-cooking techniques: a hot-smoking barbecue method and an oven method. Whichever you choose, the result will be a plateful of ribs with tender meat and a sticky, caramelized sauce.

MAKE IT
extraordinary

Korean gochujang gives the sticky ribs' sauce extra spiciness and umami.

1-1.5kg (2¼lb-3lb 3oz) meaty pork spare ribs

chopped parsley, to garnish

FOR THE SAUCE

1 tbsp clear honey

1 tbsp Dijon mustard

1 tbsp gochujang (red chilli paste)

2 tbsp cider vinegar

splash of dark soy sauce

1 tsp paprika

drizzle of olive oil

salt and freshly ground black pepper

1 To make the sauce, put the honey, mustard, gochujang, cider vinegar, soy sauce, paprika, and olive oil in a bowl. Season generously with salt and black pepper, and mix well. Smother the ribs with the sauce, then wrap tightly in foil.

2 Preheat the oven to 150°C (300°F/Gas 2). Place the foil-wrapped ribs in a roasting tin and cook for 2 hours, or until the meat pulls away from the bone and the sauce caramelizes. Unwrap the ribs, baste with the sauce, then finish under a hot grill for 5-10 minutes.

ALTERNATIVELY, if you have a barbecue with a hot-smoking setup, position hot charcoal off to one side of the barbecue and add wood chips. Use an oven thermometer to get the heat to 150°C (300°F) - it can be adjusted using the ventilation holes or by adding more charcoal. Cook the foil-wrapped ribs for 2 hours, until the meat pulls away from the bone and the sauce caramelizes. Then unwrap the ribs, baste with the sauce, and finish on the grill for another 20-30 minutes.

PREP 10 MINUTES
COOK (OVEN) 2 HOURS 10 MINUTES
COOK (BARBECUE) 2 HOURS 30 MINUTES
SERVES 4

TOAD IN THE HOLE WITH ALE AND ONION GRAVY

A grown-up take on a classic comfort-food dish, both the batter and gravy of this toad in the hole are enhanced with pale ale and fresh herbs for a more complex flavour.

3 eggs
150ml (5fl oz) pale ale
150ml (5fl oz) milk
210g (7½oz) plain flour
1 garlic clove
1 bay leaf
2 sprigs thyme
2 sprigs rosemary
salt
8 pork and leek sausages
1 tbsp vegetable oil
2 heaped tbsp duck fat

FOR THE GRAVY
50g (1¾oz) butter
splash of olive oil
1 onion, finely sliced
1 red onion, finely sliced
6 sprigs thyme, leaves picked
300ml (10fl oz) pale ale
500ml (16fl oz) chicken stock
1 tbsp wholegrain mustard
2 tbsp cornflour, mixed with
   cold water to make a paste

1 In a bowl whisk together the eggs, ale, and milk. Sift in the flour and whisk into a smooth batter. Add the bay leaf, garlic, thyme, and 1 of the rosemary sprigs, season with a little salt, and leave to rest overnight in the fridge.

2 Remove the batter from the fridge, lift out the herbs and garlic, and whisk until smooth. Set aside for 30 minutes to reach room temperature.

3 Preheat the oven to 200°C (400°F/Gas 6). Heat the oil in a frying pan and fry the sausages until golden.

4 Add the duck fat to an ovenproof dish. Place the dish in the oven for 10 minutes, until smoking hot. Remove from the oven and add the sausages and the leaves from the remaining rosemary sprig. Pour the batter over and return to the oven. Cook for 35–40 minutes, until the batter is crispy and well risen.

5 Meanwhile, make the gravy. Melt the butter and oil in a frying pan over a low heat. Add the onions and thyme leaves, and gently cook for 30 minutes, until soft and turning golden. Pour in the pale ale, increase the heat, and cook for 2–3 minutes until bubbling. Add the chicken stock and mustard. Bring to the boil and simmer for 15–20 minutes.

6 Return to the boil, add the cornflour mixture, and whisk for a few minutes, until thickened. Season with salt and serve alongside the toad in the hole.

MAKE IT *extraordinary*

Smoking-hot duck fat helps encourage the batter to rise and makes it extra crispy.

Crisp, fruity pale ale enriches the toad in the hole batter and accompanying gravy.

PREP 20 MINUTES, PLUS CHILLING
COOK 1 HOUR
SERVES 4

VEGETARIAN

TIM ANDERSON MasterChef Champion 2011

MUSHROOM AND SOBA NOODLE BOWL WITH BERGAMOT

Don't be put off by the amount of ingredients in this Japanese noodle dish – the depth of flavour they produce is far superior to any simple bowl of ramen.

Kombu is made from dried kelp, and is a key ingredient when making Japanese stock (dashi).

20g (¾oz) kombu

15g (½oz) dried shiitake mushrooms

15g (½oz) dried porcini mushrooms

4 strips bergamot (or lemon) peel

4 tbsp mirin

4 tbsp Japanese soy sauce (or more, to taste)

100g (3½oz) cornflour

1 tbsp white sesame seeds, toasted

1 tbsp black sesame seeds, toasted

1 block (300g/10oz) firm cotton tofu, cut into 8 slices

4 tbsp vegetable oil, plus 1 tsp for the mushrooms

1 bunch (150–200g/5½–7oz) enoki mushrooms, roots removed

1 bunch (150–200g/5½–7oz) shimeji (beech) mushrooms

100g (3½oz) fresh spinach

4 eggs

300–400g (10–14oz) soba noodles

2 spring onions, finely sliced

4 pinches toasted white sesame seeds

shichimi togarashi (Japanese spice blend), to serve

1 To make the broth, rinse the kombu in cold water, and add to a saucepan with 1.2 litres (2 pints) of water, the dried mushrooms, and bergamot peel. Over a medium heat, gradually bring to a very low simmer, then remove from the heat and leave to infuse for 30 minutes, stirring occasionally to ensure the mushrooms are submerged. Pass through a sieve, extracting as much liquid as possible. Discard the kombu and the peel. Thinly slice the shiitake and porcini, removing the shiitake stems if tough, and set aside. Add the mirin and soy sauce to the broth, adding more soy sauce if needed.

2 Mix together the cornflour and sesame seeds. Dredge the tofu in this mixture to coat on all sides. Heat 4 tbsp oil in a frying pan over a medium-high heat, then add the tofu and cook for 3–4 minutes on each side, until golden brown. Drain on kitchen paper. Wipe the pan clean, add the remaining oil, then return to the heat. Sauté the mushrooms, including the shiitake and porcini, until just tender.

3 Boil the eggs for 6 minutes, then remove and place in a container of cold water. Peel the eggs and halve them. Blanch the spinach in the water for a few seconds, then remove and drain well.

4 Heat the broth to a low simmer. Cook the soba noodles in a separate saucepan, according to the packet instructions. When they are almost done, ladle the broth into deep bowls. Drain the noodles and add to the bowls, then top with the fried tofu, mushrooms, spinach, eggs, and spring onions. Finish with a pinch of sesame seeds and shichimi togarashi.

Shichimi togarashi can include chilli pepper, sansho pepper, ginger, and sesame seeds.

PREP 30 MINUTES
COOK 50 MINUTES
SERVES 4

BUTTERNUT AND ALMOND PESTO LASAGNE STACKS

This vegetable lasagne uses Japanese-style dumpling wrappers instead of pasta sheets to create neat layers of butternut squash, tomato sauce, and almond pesto.

MAKE IT
extraordinary

Dumpling or gyoza wrappers are used instead of pasta to create thin, crisp, even lasagne layers.

1 small butternut squash, peeled and cut into 1cm (½in) dice

1 tbsp olive oil

salt and black pepper

40 dumpling wrappers

60g (2oz) vegetarian Parmesan cheese, finely grated

FOR THE BASIL OIL

100g (3½oz) basil

75ml (2½fl oz) groundnut oil

FOR THE TOMATO SAUCE

400g can chopped tomatoes

100g (3½oz) cherry tomatoes

3 garlic cloves, roasted

½ bunch of basil, chopped

1 tsp red wine vinegar

pinch of sugar

FOR THE PESTO

50g (1¾oz) almonds, skin on

50g (1¾oz) vegetarian Parmesan cheese

juice of 1 lemon

1 garlic clove, grated

100ml (3½fl oz) olive oil

1 bunch basil

FOR THE CHEESE SAUCE

80g (3oz) mascarpone

3 tbsp double cream

25g (scant 1oz) vegetarian Parmesan cheese, grated

juice of ½ lemon

1 First, make the basil oil (see p250) and set aside. Preheat the oven to 180°C (350°F/Gas 4). Place the squash in a baking tray, drizzle with a little olive oil, season with salt, and roast for 20 minutes, until it starts to soften. Remove from the oven and allow to cool. Leave the oven on. Make the tomato sauce (see p152), then set it aside until ready to serve.

2 Meanwhile, place a non-stick frying pan over a medium heat. Spoon one-quarter of the Parmesan in the pan and cook gently for 3–5 minutes until the cheese melts and becomes golden. Transfer the tuile to baking parchment and roll out thinly with a rolling pin. Repeat with the remaining cheese. Set aside.

3 For the pesto, place the almonds on a baking sheet and roast for 3–4 minutes in the oven until they start to release oil. Remove from the oven and allow to cool, then put in a food processor with the remaining pesto ingredients and process until almost smooth. Season with salt and set aside.

4 Make the cheese sauce by whisking the mascarpone with the double cream in a bowl. Add the Parmesan and season with a little salt and lemon juice. Set aside.

5 Preheat the oven to 200°C (400°F/Gas 6). Lay 4 dumpling wrappers in a ceramic baking dish. Place 1 tsp of tomato sauce on each, drizzle with ½ tsp of pesto, and add 4–5 cubes of squash. Repeat until 10 layers high. On the top layer, add the same amount of tomato sauce and pesto, then divide the cheese sauce mixture between the 4 stacks. Bake in the oven for 20–25 minutes, until golden and a little crispy. Serve each lasagne with a drizzle of basil oil and a Parmesan tuile.

Substitute almonds for pine nuts in this fresh pesto that pairs well with butternut squash.

PREP 40 MINUTES
COOK 1 HOUR 40 MINUTES
SERVES 4

MAURITIAN VEGAN BURGERS

This plant-based burger is full of flavour, with a curry powder and cumin-spiced patty, and a light, fragrant mint and coriander chutney.

200g (7oz) cooked mashed potatoes

50g (1¾oz) cooked peas

2 tsp curry powder

1 tsp ground cumin

2 tbsp chopped coriander leaves

1 tbsp chopped parsley

1 tbsp mango chutney

salt

oil, for frying

MINT CORIANDER CHUTNEY

15g (½oz) mint, plus extra to serve

30g (1oz) coriander, plus extra to serve

1 garlic clove

juice of 1 lime

3 tbsp oil

TO SERVE

4 buns

tomato ketchup

sliced tomatoes

shredded lettuce

1 Combine the potato, peas, spices, herbs, and mango chutney in a large bowl and mash until combined. Season with salt to taste. Shape the mixture into 4 equal-sized patties and place on a plate lined with baking parchment. Chill for 30 minutes to firm up.

2 Meanwhile, place all the ingredients for the chutney in a food processor or blender. Add 4–5 tsp of hot water and process into a smooth green sauce. Set aside.

3 Heat enough oil to cover the base of a large non-stick frying pan. Fry the burgers over a moderate heat for 6–7 minutes on each side, until golden brown. Drain on kitchen paper.

4 Preheat the grill. Toast the buns under the grill, then spread a layer of the mint chutney and tomato ketchup over the bases. Place the burgers on the bun bases and top with some sliced tomatoes, a few mint and coriander leaves, and shredded lettuce. Add the bun tops and serve.

Mango chutney adds a tangy sweetness to the burgers.

Cumin and curry powder pack the burgers full of flavour and colour.

PREP 15 MINUTES, PLUS CHILLING
COOK 10 MINUTES
SERVES 4

MUSHROOM AND TRUFFLE RISOTTO

Enrich vegetarian mushroom risotto, a hearty, satisfying Italian classic, with the addition of intensely flavoured truffle paste. Use it sparingly – just a teaspoon's worth will work wonders.

MAKE IT
extraordinary

More intense than oil, truffle paste contains real truffle pieces and has a rich, heady flavour.

6 tbsp olive oil

4 garlic cloves (whole and skin on, crushed with your palm)

5–6 sprigs of thyme

2 litres (3½ pints) hot vegetable stock

100g (3½oz) cold butter, cut into cubes

250g (9oz) chestnut mushrooms, roughly chopped

250g (9oz) white mushrooms, finely sliced

2 banana shallots, very finely chopped

550g (1¼lb) Arborio rice

250ml (9fl oz) white wine

1 tsp truffle paste

2 tsp freshly ground black pepper

large handful of flat-leaf parsley, finely chopped

125g (4½oz) vegetarian Parmesan cheese, grated

1 Heat half of the oil with the garlic cloves and thyme in a large heavy-based saucepan over a medium heat. Add the chestnut mushrooms and fry for 10–15 minutes, until golden. Remove from the heat and discard the garlic and thyme. Whizz the mushrooms in a blender until smooth, with a ladleful of the hot stock.

2 Heat half of the butter in the same pan and, when foaming, add the white mushrooms and a pinch of salt and pepper. Fry for 10–15 minutes, until the mushrooms start to colour. Remove with a slotted spoon and set aside.

3 Add the remaining oil to the pan and fry the shallots for 10–12 minutes, until translucent and starting to colour.

4 Add the rice and stir well, then add the wine and cook until it has almost evaporated. Add 150ml (5fl oz) of the stock and cook over a low heat, stirring occasionally, until the stock has been absorbed by the rice. Add more stock, 150ml (5fl oz) at a time, until the rice is cooked, allowing each addition to be absorbed before adding the next.

5 Remove from the heat and stir through the truffle paste, mushroom purée, remaining butter, and the sautéed mushrooms. Stir until the butter has melted and absorbed into the risotto.

6 Stir through the pepper, parsley, and half the vegetarian Parmesan. Serve sprinkled with the remaining Parmesan.

PREP 10 MINUTES
COOK 1 HOUR
SERVES 8

BUTTERNUT SQUASH TAGINE BAKED IN A WHOLE PUMPKIN

Baking this vegetarian classic inside a whole pumpkin not only looks great on the table: it also keeps the spicy tagine moist and tender.

MAKE IT *extraordinary*

Pine nuts, coriander, and olive oil make a fragrant, crunchy dressing for the tagine.

1 pumpkin (about 3kg/6½lbs)

sea salt and freshly ground black pepper

4 tbsp light olive oil

2 red onions, finely chopped

1 large red pepper, deseeded and diced

4 garlic cloves, chopped

1 thumb-sized piece of fresh root ginger, finely chopped

1 tsp chilli powder

2 tsp ground coriander

1 tbsp ground cumin

1 tbsp garam masala

2 x 400g can chopped tomatoes

700ml (1 pint) vegetable stock

2 tbsp clear honey

200g (7oz) diced butternut squash

200g (7oz) canned chickpeas

150g (5½oz) Basmati rice

100g (3½oz) dried apricots, chopped

FOR THE OIL

100g (3½oz) coriander sprigs

180ml (6fl oz) extra virgin olive oil

3 tbsp pine nuts

1 tsp cumin seeds

1 Preheat the oven to 200°C (400°F/Gas 6). Cut a "lid" out of the top of the pumpkin, reserving it for later. Scrape out the pumpkin seeds and fibrous flesh and season with sea salt. Scrunch up a double layer of foil on a baking tray, forming a nest to hold the pumpkin steady. Sit the pumpkin on top.

2 Heat the olive oil in a large saucepan over a low heat. Add the onions, red pepper, garlic, and ginger, and fry for 2 minutes, until softened but not brown. Add the spices and continue to cook for another 2 minutes over a low heat, to release their aroma. Add the tomatoes, stock, and honey, then season well with salt and pepper. Bring to the boil, then reduce to a low simmer and cook, uncovered, for 30 minutes.

3 Add the butternut squash, chickpeas, rice, and apricots, and mix well. Add more water if it looks a little dry. Check the seasoning and continue cooking for 10 minutes. Pour the mixture into the pumpkin, replace the lid, and bake for 1-1¼ hours, until both the pumpkin and squash are tender.

4 In the meantime, make the oil. Purée the coriander leaves and stalks with the oil in a small blender. Pour through a fine sieve into a jug, pressing to extract as much of the oil as possible. Discard the solids. In a small frying pan, toast the pine nuts and cumin seeds over a medium heat until the pine nuts start to brown. Mix the nuts and oil together and set aside.

5 Carefully remove the foil and place the whole pumpkin on a platter. Serve with the pine nut oil to drizzle over.

Garam masala spices give this typically North African dish a South Asian flavour.

PREP 15 MINUTES
COOK 2 HOURS 5 MINUTES
SERVES 4

MOUSSAKA-STUFFED AUBERGINES

Instead of putting aubergines in a moussaka, why not put moussaka inside an aubergine? Serve a few small stuffed aubergines drizzled with fresh dill oil.

Vivid green dill oil adds a pop of colour around the stuffed, baked aubergines.

Delicate, bright microgreens decorate the plate and add bursts of flavour.

splash of olive oil
1 large carrot, finely diced
1 onion, finely diced
1 celery stick, finely diced
2 garlic cloves, crushed
½ tsp ground cinnamon
½ tsp ground allspice
½ tsp ground cumin
1 tsp dried oregano
1 tbsp tomato purée
100ml (3½fl oz) red wine
400g can chopped tomatoes
100ml (3½fl oz) vegetable stock
400g can chickpeas, rinsed and drained
pinch of sugar
1 tsp red wine vinegar
salt
12 small aubergines
microgreens, for garnish

FOR THE DILL OIL
75ml (2½fl oz) groundnut oil
100g (3½oz) dill

FOR THE BÉCHAMEL SAUCE
25g (scant 1oz) unsalted butter
25g (scant 1oz) plain flour
300ml (10fl oz) milk
pinch of nutmeg
50g (1¾oz) feta cheese, crumbled
25g (scant 1oz) vegetarian Parmesan cheese, grated
50g (1¾oz) ricotta cheese
1 egg yolk

1 First, make the dill oil. Add the oil to a small pan and heat to 80°C (175°F). Remove from the heat, then carefully pour into a blender, add the dill, and blitz until smooth. Strain the oil, discarding any solids, then set aside until ready to serve.

2 Make the béchamel sauce: melt the butter in a saucepan, remove from the heat, and whisk in the flour. Cook over a low heat for 3–4 minutes, then slowly add the milk, whisking continuously. When the mixture starts to thicken, add the nutmeg and cheeses, then season with salt. Allow to thicken a little more, then remove from the heat, mix in the egg yolk, and set aside.

3 Make the filling. In a large saucepan, heat the olive oil and sweat the carrot, onion, and celery for about 10 minutes, until softened. Add the garlic, spices, oregano, and tomato purée, and cook for another 2 minutes. Add the red wine and cook for another 2 minutes, then add the chopped tomatoes and stock. Bring to the boil and reduce to a simmer. Add the chickpeas, sugar, and vinegar, and cook for 10 minutes, until thickened slightly. Season with salt to taste and set aside.

4 Preheat the oven to 180°C (350°F/Gas 4). Slice the top 2cm (¾in) off the aubergines, then trim a little off the bottom of each so they sit upright. Scoop out the flesh, leaving a 1cm (½in) wall, with about 2.5cm (1in) at the bottom. Season inside with salt. Spoon in the filling three-quarters of the way up each aubergine, then top with béchamel sauce, reserving about one-third for later. Stand the aubergines in a non-stick ceramic baking dish. Bake for 45–50 minutes.

5 Remove from the oven and spoon over the reserved sauce. Place under a medium grill until the sauce is golden. Serve with a drizzle of dill oil and garnish with microgreens.

PREP 25 MINUTES
COOK 1 HOUR 40 MINUTES
SERVES 4

MEDITERRANEAN VEGETABLE AND TOFU COUSCOUS CAKES

This recipe turns a simple vegetable couscous side into a meal in its own right. Serve 3–4 patties with the fruity yogurt dressing as a light lunch, or fry up a whole batch to serve as finger food at a summer party.

1 small or ½ large aubergine, cut into 1cm (½in) cubes

1 red pepper, cut into 1cm (½in) cubes

1 courgette, cut into 1cm (½in) cubes

1 red onion, cut into 1cm (½in) cubes

3½ tbsp olive oil

1 tsp ground cumin

salt and freshly ground black pepper

300g (10oz) couscous

1 tbsp vegetable stock powder

200g (7oz) firm tofu, mashed

1 garlic clove, minced

2 eggs, beaten

120g (4½ oz) fresh breadcrumbs

vegetable oil, for shallow frying

FOR THE DRESSING

seeds from 1 pomegranate

handful mint leaves, finely chopped, plus a few whole to garnish

handful flat-leaf parsley leaves, finely chopped, plus a few whole to garnish

200g (7oz) Greek-style yogurt

juice of 1 lemon

¼ tsp ground turmeric

1 Preheat the oven to 200°C (400°F/Gas 6). Put the aubergine, red pepper, courgette, and red onion in a large roasting tray and toss with the cumin and 2 tbsp of the olive oil. Season well with salt and pepper, spread them out in a single layer, and cook at the top of the oven for 30–40 minutes, turning once, until tender and browned at the edges. Remove from the oven and allow to cool.

2 Boil a kettle. Put the couscous into a large, shallow bowl and drizzle over the remaining 1½ tbsp olive oil. Scatter with the vegetable stock powder and mix it in with a fork. Pour about 525ml (17fl oz) of boiling water over the couscous, making sure it is just covered, and stir briefly with a fork. Immediately cover the bowl with a tight layer of cling film and leave to steam for 5 minutes. Remove the cling film and check the grains are nearly soft and all the water absorbed. Fork over to loosen the grains.

3 In a large bowl, mix together the vegetables, couscous, tofu, garlic, eggs, and breadcrumbs. Season with salt and pepper. Mould into 5cm (2in) patties and refrigerate for 10–15 minutes to firm up. Mix together all the yogurt dressing ingredients, reserving a few pomegranate seeds to garnish, and set aside.

4 Heat 1 tbsp vegetable oil in a frying pan, and fry the cakes over a medium heat until browned on both sides. Serve hot with the yogurt dressing, garnished with pomegranate seeds and mint leaves.

Mint leaves give the dressing a light and fragrant tang.

Fresh pomegranate seeds add a sour-sweet pop of flavour to the yogurt dressing.

PREP 15 MINUTES, PLUS CHILLING
COOK 50 MINUTES
SERVES 8

SPICED TOMATO AND GRUYÈRE TARTLETS WITH FENNEL JAM

The inclusion of fennel and nigella seeds gives these tomato tartlets a unique flavour. The jam can be made 1-2 weeks in advance and kept in the fridge.

2 tbsp light olive oil

6 large, very ripe tomatoes, diced

salt and freshly ground black pepper

2 tsp fennel seeds

2 tsp nigella seeds

400g (14oz) puff pastry

flour, for dusting

3 medium tomatoes, thinly sliced and lightly salted to draw out some moisture

1 tbsp olive oil

150g (5½oz) vegetarian Gruyère cheese, grated

rocket and watercress, to serve

FOR THE JAM

25g (scant 1oz) unsalted butter

1 fennel bulb, sliced extremely finely (ideally with a mandolin)

1 white onion, thinly sliced

150g (5½oz) soft brown sugar

100ml (3½fl oz) malt vinegar

2 tsp fennel seeds

1 For the jam, melt the butter in a heavy-based pan, then add the remaining jam ingredients. Bring to the boil, reduce the heat and cook gently for 30-40 minutes, stirring occasionally, until all the liquid has evaporated.

2 Preheat the oven to 200°C (400°F/Gas 6). Place a medium saucepan over a high heat, add the olive oil and the diced tomatoes, and cover immediately. After 5 minutes, add a good pinch of salt and pepper. Continue to cook, uncovered, stirring every few minutes. When the sauce has thickened, pass through a sieve, stir in half the fennel and nigella seeds, and set aside.

3 Roll out the pastry on a floured work surface into a large rectangle or square about 5mm (¼in) thick. Scatter with the remaining fennel and nigella seeds, fold in half, and roll out to its full size again. Cut into quarters.

4 Lay each pastry on a baking tray, then use a sharp knife to score a border about 2cm (¾in) in from the edges all the way around, being careful not to cut all the way through. Using the back of the knife, score the pastry around the outer edges - this will help it to puff up.

5 Add 1-2 tbsp of sauce to each pastry, keeping inside the border. Sprinkle over half of the Gruyère, then arrange the sliced tomatoes on top and scatter over the remaining cheese.

6 Bake in the oven for about 20 minutes, or until the pastry is cooked and golden. Serve hot, accompanied by the fennel jam and a salad of peppery rocket and watercress.

Fennel seeds add an aniseed note to the tarts, complementing the accompanying jam.

Slightly bitter and onion-like, nigella seeds balance out the tomato sauce's sweetness.

PREP 25 MINUTES
COOK 1 HOUR 15 MINUTES
SERVES 4

SALIHA MAHMOOD AHMED
Champion 2017

My name is Saliha and I won *MasterChef* in 2017. Since the show, I've written my first cookbook, and taken part in cookery demonstrations across the country – all while being a doctor, wife, and mother.

Q What's your favourite moment from your time on the show?

A Winning – but that's too simple. My second favourite moment would be being in South Africa. The heat was just horrible and we were doing barbecues at midday – it was crazy and I don't know how we managed to get through it, but we did.

Q What was the first recipe you really made your own?

A The rose-scented chicken I made for the critics on *MasterChef*. They really liked it. I'm very passionate about that dish, because I think it brought lots of different elements of my food culture together, and its success gave me so much confidence going forward.

Q Best meal of the day: breakfast, lunch, or dinner?

A I'm always in such a rush that I never have breakfast. Lunch is usually in the hospital canteen or something quick, so it has to be dinner. I come home from work, give myself half an hour of me time, and then make a nice meal for me, my husband, and my little one.

Q What was your worst kitchen moment?

A I was making a lassi, and accidentally left the lid off the blender. Suddenly there was yogurt everywhere. My kitchen still smells a bit yogurty.

Q What's your favourite ingredient and why?

A Rosewater – I put it in everything. I don't think we use floral scents enough. I like to wear flowers, I like to smell of roses, and I like rose in my food.

Q Who are your biggest food heroes and why?

A Growing up, I loved Jamie Oliver, Nigella Lawson, and Anjum Anand. I love Sabrina Ghayour's writing, and all the authors writing about Central Asian, Persian, Pakistani, and Indian cookery.

Q Any advice for potential MasterChefs?

A Relax and take it easy. At the end of the day, you're doing what you love, so why stress? Do it in as relaxed a way as you can and you're likely to get the best outcome.

SMOKED LABNEH, SLOW-ROASTED TOMATO, AND POMEGRANATE SALAD

Labneh is a thick, creamy Middle Eastern soft cheese that can be made at home with Greek yogurt. Use it instead of halloumi in this fresh, vibrant summer salad.

FOR THE LABNEH
250g (9oz) Greek-style yogurt (10 per cent fat)
2 tsp honey
1 tsp olive oil
pinch of sea salt
50g (1¾oz) oolong tea
peel of 2 limes
1 dried lime, roughly chopped
Turkish bread, to serve

FOR THE TOMATOES
4 tomatoes, on the vine
2 tbsp extra virgin olive oil
1 tbsp sherry vinegar
1 tsp rose harissa
1 tsp pomegranate molasses
1 tsp sea salt

FOR THE DRESSING
juice of 1 lime
3 tbsp olive oil
1 tomato on the vine, finely diced, seeds included
3 tbsp pomegranate seeds

FOR THE SALAD
50g (1¾oz) rocket leaves
handful of coarsely chopped flat-leaf parsley
handful of tarragon leaves
1 small Lebanese cucumber, peeled, deseeded, and diced

1 For the labneh, mix the yogurt, honey, olive oil, and salt in a bowl. Transfer to to a clean J-cloth, bring the edges together, and fasten with a rubber band. Hang in the fridge over a bowl for 12–24 hours, for the liquid to drain.

2 Prepare the roasted tomatoes. Preheat the oven to 120°C (250°F/Gas ½). Mix the oil, sherry, rose harissa, molasses, and salt in a bowl. Halve the tomatoes lengthways and toss in the mixture to coat. Place the tomatoes cut-side up on a metal rack over a baking tray. Roast for 2½–3 hours, until the tomatoes have shrunk slightly, but retain a moist centre. Remove from the oven and allow to cool completely.

3 Remove the labneh from the cloth and place it on a piece of baking parchment. Line the base of a large flameproof roasting tin with a large piece of foil. Place the tea, lime peel, and dried lime on the foil with 1 tbsp of water. Set the tin over a very high heat. When it begins to smoke, place a wire rack in the roasting tin, place the labneh on its paper on top, and cover the whole tin with plenty of foil to seal in the smoke. Remove from the heat and leave the tin to stand for about 30 minutes. Remove the labneh and return it to the fridge.

4 To assemble the salad, mix all the dressing ingredients in a small jug and stir well to combine. Place the rocket, parsley, tarragon, and cucumber on a wide serving platter. Scatter over the dressing, followed by the roasted tomatoes and spoonfuls of the chilled smoked labneh. Serve with toasted crusty Turkish bread.

MAKE IT
extraordinary

The homemade smoked labneh takes on the rich, complex flavours of oolong tea.

Dress the tomatoes in rose harissa: a hot spice mix with delicate floral notes.

Tart pomegranate seeds contrast with the smoky labneh and echo the flavour of the molasses.

PREP 10 MINUTES
COOK 40 MINUTES, PLUS DRAINING AND COOLING
SERVES 4

PASTA PRIMAVERA WITH COURGETTE FLOWERS

Lend a touch of summer to this springtime pasta dish with bright-yellow courgette strips and rich, deep-fried courgette flowers stuffed with cheese and fresh herbs.

Sweet yellow courgettes contrast with the red and green vegetables in this dish.

Stuff courgette flowers with a herby ricotta mix and deep-fry them for a seasonal topping.

100g (3½oz) double-podded broad beans

bunch of fine asparagus spears, trimmed and cut diagonally into 3–4cm (1½in) pieces

350g (12oz) dried spaghetti

2 tbsp olive oil, plus extra to serve

1 garlic clove, very finely sliced

1 yellow courgette, cut into strips with a mandolin

2 tbsp finely chopped parsley leaves

2 tbsp finely chopped basil leaves

1 tbsp finely chopped tarragon leaves

100g (3½oz) ripe cherry tomatoes, halved

juice of ½ lemon

vegetarian Parmesan cheese shavings, to serve

FOR THE COURGETTE FLOWERS

100g (3½oz) ricotta

25g (scant 1oz) vegetarian Parmesan cheese, grated

2–3 tbsp chopped herbs (chives, basil, parsley, basil, tarragon)

10–12 courgette flowers

vegetable oil, for deep frying

75g (2½oz) self-raising flour

100g (3½oz) cornflour

200ml (7fl oz) ice-cold fizzy water

1 Place the broad beans and asparagus in a pan of salted boiling water and cook for 2–3 minutes, until tender but still with some bite. Drain, then refresh in iced water and set aside.

2 Prepare the stuffed courgette flowers. Mix the cheeses and herbs in a bowl and season. Carefully stuff the flowers with 1–2 tsp of the mixture, and twists the ends to seal. Set aside.

3 Heat the oil to 180–190°C (350–375°F). Make a batter by sieving the flours into a bowl, then whisking in the water to reach a consistency between single and double cream. Dip the flowers in the batter to coat, and fry for 2–2½ minutes, until golden and crunchy. Keep warm while cooking the pasta.

4 Cook the spaghetti in a large saucepan of salted boiling water, according to the packet instructions. Meanwhile, heat the olive oil in a large frying pan, add the garlic and cook for 30 seconds, then add the courgette, season, and cook for 3–4 minutes, until the courgette turns golden. Add the broad beans, asparagus, and tomatoes to the frying pan. Stir and cook over a low heat for 2–3 minutes.

5 Drain the spaghetti, then add to the frying pan with a little of the cooking water, and toss with the vegetables to combine. Stir in the herbs and add a squeeze of lemon juice.

6 Using a carving fork or 2 chopsticks, twist a quarter of the spaghetti into a neat nest, and place on a plate. Drizzle over a little olive oil and serve with the courgette flowers and Parmesan shavings.

PREP 35 MINUTES
COOK 25 MINUTES
SERVES 4

GATO PIMENT

In Mauritius, our equivalent of falafel is a type of chilli cake known as gato piment. Made with yellow split peas, it is a lot lighter in texture than falafel. It is also ridiculously moreish, and is the biggest-selling dish at my restaurant.

200g (7oz) yellow split peas, soaked in cold water overnight

2 bird's-eye chillies, finely chopped

2 garlic cloves, finely chopped

2 tbsp finely chopped coriander leaves

2 tbsp finely chopped mint leaves

1 spring onion, finely chopped

1 tsp ground turmeric

salt

vegetable oil for frying

1 Drain the yellow split peas in batches, reserving the liquid. Place in a food processor and pulse until they resemble mashed potatoes in texture. If the mixture is too dry, add a little of the soaking liquid.

2 Transfer the mixture to a bowl, add in all the remaining ingredients, season with salt, and stir well to combine.

3 Heat 10cm (4in) of oil in a deep wok. With wet hands, take a teaspoon of the mixture, roll it into a ball, and drop it straight into the wok. Fry in batches for 3-4 minutes, until lightly golden, then drain on kitchen paper. Repeat for the remaining mixture. Serve immediately.

Turmeric enhances the colour of the split peas, turning the gato piment a vivid yellow.

Just as chickpeas are used for falafel, yellow split peas are the main ingredient of gato piment.

PREP 10 MINUTES, PLUS SOAKING
COOK 15 MINUTES
SERVES 4

PING COOMBES
Champion 2014

My name is Ping and I won *MasterChef* in 2014. I've since become the Executive Chef of Chi Kitchen, written a cookbook, launched a YouTube channel, and travelled around the world to promote Malaysian food.

Q What's your favourite moment from the show and why?

A There are too many... but of course the moment that I found out I had won is the most special of them all.

Q What was the first recipe you made your own?

A My take on chicken and sweetcorn soup. I made a pan-fried chicken with creamy sweetcorn velouté, and I wanted it to be sweet and salty, so I added some bacon. Also, I thought it needed some colour as it was all very brown and yellow, so I added purple potatoes. People say never use purple potatoes, but I thought why not? The dish tasted and looked great.

Q What is your worst kitchen moment?

A I remember my worst moment on *MasterChef* so well. I made this bowl of laksa, which didn't have much broth in it but was really intense. I was very proud of it – it was a show-stopper. Unfortunately, when I turned around I moved too quickly and the whole bowl fell to the floor. I remember the silence in the studio as everyone scrambled to find me another bowl.

Q What's your favourite ingredient or kitchen tool?

A My favourite ingredient is lemongrass. It's so versatile, and can be used in savoury food and desserts. I love it so much that it is on the front cover of my cookbook. My favourite piece of equipment is my food processor. It does everything for me and I use it almost every day.

Q Who is your biggest food hero and why?

A My food hero has to be my mother. She encourages me to cook with my heart and soul and put a lot of love into my food.

Q Best meal of the day: breakfast, lunch, or dinner?

A My favourite meal is dinner. I make a conscious effort to make sure the whole family eats together, whatever time it is.

Q Any advice for potential MasterChefs?

A Just take the risk, because you never know what's around the corner. If you do get onto *MasterChef*, go for it, and don't hold back: you've got one chance and you need to make the best of it.

NO-COOK RAINBOW PAD THAI

Unlike a typical pad Thai, this noodle dish does not need to be stir-fried. As a result, the carrot ribbons, beansprouts, and shredded cabbage remain crunchy and almost salad-like, while the dressing makes sure the dish remains hot in flavour, if not in temperature.

250g (9oz) wide or medium rice noodles

vegetable oil, to coat

1 carrot, shredded

¼ red cabbage, shredded

100g (3½oz) beansprouts

bunch of spring onions, trimmed and finely chopped

small handful coriander leaves, chopped, plus extra to garnish

75g (2½oz) dry-roasted peanuts, roughly chopped

FOR THE DRESSING

1 garlic clove, grated

1 tbsp grated ginger

juice of 1 lime

1 tbsp vegetarian "fish sauce" (optional)

2 tsp tamarind paste

1 tbsp honey

1 tbsp light soy sauce

1 tbsp sriracha

½ tsp sesame oil

2 tbsp smooth peanut butter

1 Soak the noodles in boiling water for 10–15 minutes until soft. Drain and run under cold water. Drizzle with a little vegetable oil to coat the noodles so that they don't stick.

2 Place the noodles in a large bowl with the carrot, red cabbage, beansprouts, spring onions, and coriander.

3 Combine all the dressing ingredients in a small bowl and whisk well to combine. Season to taste.

4 Pour the dressing onto the noodles and vegetables and toss thoroughly. The best way to make sure they are well incorporated is to use your hands to massage the noodles with the dressing.

5 Serve with the chopped peanuts on top and a scattering of coriander leaves to garnish.

MAKE IT *extraordinary*

Always use freshly grated ginger rather than pre-made paste.

Sour-tasting tamarind paste is balanced by the honey in the pad Thai dressing.

Sriracha hot sauce adds an instant kick to the dressing.

PREP 25 MINUTES
SERVES 4

THAI RED CURRY TEMPURA MEDLEY

Deconstruct a vegetarian curry by deep-frying tofu and tempura-battered vegetable pieces, then serve on a bed of creamy Thai red curry sauce.

MAKE IT
extraordinary

Try making your own Thai red curry paste – see p47.

100g (3½oz) sweet potatoes, cut into bite-sized pieces

vegetable oil, for deep-frying

200g (7oz) firm tofu, cut into small cubes

100g (3½oz) broccoli, cut into bite-sized pieces

100g (3½oz) asparagus, cut into bite-sized pieces

100g (3½oz) cauliflower florets, thinly sliced, to serve

5 red radishes, thinly sliced, to serve

FOR THE SAUCE

2 tbsp Thai red curry paste

200ml (7fl oz) can coconut milk

200ml (7fl oz) coconut cream

2 tbsp palm sugar or demerara sugar

2 tbsp mushroom soy sauce or light soy sauce

1 tsp tamarind concentrate

FOR THE BATTER

85g (3oz) plain flour

1 tbsp cornflour

½ tsp ground turmeric

¼ tsp salt

200ml (7fl oz) ice-cold sparkling water

1 To make the sauce, place the curry paste in a large frying pan or wok over a medium-high heat, and cook, stirring, for a few seconds. Add the coconut milk and cream, and bring to a gentle boil, stirring occasionally, then cook for 2–3 minutes, until the sauce releases its aroma. Add the sugar, soy sauce, and tamarind, and season to taste. Simmer and let the sauce reduce for about 15 minutes, until it coats the back of a spoon. Remove from the heat.

2 Preheat the oven to 150°C (300°F/Gas 2). Bring a pan of water fitted with a steamer basket to the boil. Add the sweet potato and steam for 5 minutes, then set aside.

3 Heat the oil in a deep-fat fryer or a medium saucepan to 190°C (375°F). Fry the tofu for 5 minutes, until crispy. Drain on kitchen paper and keep warm in the oven, leaving the oven door slightly ajar.

4 Whisk the batter ingredients together (do not worry if there are a few lumps). Dip pieces of broccoli, asparagus, and steamed sweet potato in the batter, shake off the excess, then fry in batches. Avoid overcrowding the pan. Keep the vegetables warm in the oven until ready to serve.

5 When all the tempura vegetables have been deep-fried, heat up the curry sauce. Put 4–5 tbsp of sauce on each plate, and top with a selection of tempura, followed by the crispy tofu, raw cauliflower, and radish.

PREP 30 MINUTES
COOK 20 MINUTES
SERVES 4

SMOKY AUBERGINE PARMIGIANA ARANCINI

Inspired by the the classic Italian baked aubergine dish, this recipe combines the ingredients of a parmigiana inside crisp and filling arancini (deep-fried risotto balls).

MAKE IT *extraordinary*

Charring the skin of the aubergine gives the flesh an intense, smoky flavour.

2 aubergines
25g (scant 1oz) butter
splash of olive oil
1 onion, finely diced
1 celery stick, finely diced
leaves from 5 thyme sprigs
1 bay leaf
400g (14oz) risotto rice
100ml (3½fl oz) white wine
1.8 litres (3 pints) of hot
 vegetable stock
1 mozzarella ball, chopped into
 small pieces
20g (¾oz) vegetarian Parmesan
 cheese, finely grated
salt
50g (1¾oz) plain flour
2 eggs, beaten
200g (7oz) panko breadcrumbs
2 litres vegetable oil, for deep
 frying
micro herbs, to garnish (optional)

FOR THE TOMATO SAUCE
100g (3½oz) vine cherry
 tomatoes
3 garlic cloves, peeled
½ tbsp olive oil
400g can chopped tomatoes
1 tsp red wine vinegar
pinch of sugar
½ bunch of basil, chopped

FOR THE BASIL OIL
100g (3½oz) basil
75ml (2½fl oz) groundnut oil

1 Make the basil oil (see p250) and set aside. To make the tomato sauce, preheat the oven to 180°C (350°F/Gas 4). Place the tomatoes, garlic, and oil in a roasting tin and cook for 20 minutes. Remove the tomatoes from the vine and put them into a saucepan with the garlic, chopped tomatoes, vinegar, and sugar. Simmer for 10–15 minutes until everything has infused and thickened slightly. Add the basil, season, then blitz until smooth with a hand-held blender. Set aside until ready to serve.

2 Preheat the oven to 180°C (350°F/Gas 4). With a blowtorch or gas hob, char the skin of the aubergine, then place on a lined baking tray and bake for 30–35 minutes, until soft inside.

3 Meanwhile, melt the butter with a splash of olive oil in a large saucepan. Add the onion, celery, thyme, and bay leaf, and cook for about 10 minutes until soft, stirring occasionally. Add the rice and cook, stirring, for 2–3 minutes until coated. Pour in the wine and cook for another 2 minutes. Add a ladle of hot stock to the rice, and stir in. Gradually add the rest of the stock, a ladleful at a time as it is absorbed by the rice, stirring gently so the risotto does not stick. Slice the cooked aubergine in half lengthways and scrape out the flesh. Discard the skin. Mash or blitz the flesh until smooth, then add to the cooked risotto along with the cheeses. Season with salt to taste, then set aside to cool.

4 Heat the oil in a deep-fat fryer to 180°C (350°F). Divide the risotto into 4 grapefruit-sized balls and roll in the flour, egg, and breadcrumbs. Fry for 6–7 minutes, until golden. To serve, spread tomato sauce on each plate, drizzle around some basil oil, place an arancini on top and garnish with micro herbs (if using).

A light drizzle of basil oil settles around the tomato sauce, creating a bright green outline.

PREP 40 MINUTES
COOK 1 HOUR 15 MINUTES
SERVES 4

SIDE DISHES

LENTIL, AUBERGINE, OKRA, AND NEW POTATO DHAL

This dhal recipe comes packed with a hearty assortment of vegetables that add colour, flavour, and bite to this classic Indian vegetarian dish.

MAKE IT
extraordinary

Fried aubergine adds colour, and carries the flavours of the spices well.

Okra adds an extra note of vivid colour to the dhal, and its sap also helps to thicken the dish.

5cm (2in) piece fresh root ginger

8 garlic cloves

7 tbsp vegetable oil

1 large onion, finely chopped

1 tsp fennel seeds

1 tsp nigella seeds

1 tsp ground turmeric

2 tsp ground coriander

1 tsp chilli powder

2 tbsp tomato purée

200g (7oz) red lentils, picked over and rinsed

1.4 litres (2½ pints) vegetable stock

1 aubergine, cut into 2cm (¾in) dice

50g (1¾oz) okra, halved lengthways

150g (5½oz) new potatoes, cooked and cut into 1cm (½in) slices

120ml (4fl oz) double cream

2 tbsp finely chopped coriander leaves

juice of ½ lemon

salt and freshly ground black pepper

1 Add the ginger and garlic to a blender with 3 tbsp vegetable oil and blitz to form a purée. Set aside 2 tbsp. (Freeze the remainder in ice-cube trays to use at a later date.)

2 Heat 2 tbsp vegetable oil in a large, deep-sided saucepan or casserole over a medium-low heat. Add the onion and cook, stirring frequently, for 10–15 minutes, until it is soft but not coloured.

3 Add 2 tbsp ginger and garlic purée and cook for a further 5 minutes. Stir in the spices and the tomato purée and cook for 2–3 minutes. If it starts to stick, add a splash of water.

4 Add the lentils and the stock. Bring to the boil, reduce the heat and simmer for 15 minutes.

5 Meanwhile, heat the remaining 2 tbsp vegetable oil in a frying pan and fry the aubergine until golden. Then add the okra and fry until golden. Add the aubergine and okra to the lentils, along with the potatoes, and cook for a further 5–10 minutes.

6 Whisk in the double cream, 1 tbsp of the chopped coriander, and the lemon juice. Season to taste, then serve, scattered with the remaining coriander.

PREP 15 MINS
COOK 50 MINS
SERVES 4

POTATO AND CELERIAC SALAD WITH BAYONNE HAM

Elevate the simple potato salad with a little inspiration from the French. Finely sliced Bayonne ham and crunchy shredded celeriac add a blend of textures, while tart cornichons give the creamy dressing a lift.

675g (1½lb) small new potatoes

salt and freshly ground black pepper

6 slices Bayonne ham, cut into strips

150g (5½oz) celeriac, peeled and julienned

1 tbsp finely chopped parsley

1 tbsp finely chopped chives

½ tbsp finely chopped tarragon

3 tbsp rapeseed oil

FOR THE DRESSING

1 shallot, very finely chopped

1 tbsp finely chopped cornichons

75ml (2½fl oz) crème fraîche

75ml (2½fl oz) mayonnaise

1 tsp wholegrain mustard

1 tsp chopped anchovies (optional)

1 tsp lemon juice

1 Place the potatoes in a large pan, cover with cold water, add ½ tsp salt, and bring to the boil over a high heat. Reduce the heat, cover, and simmer for 12–15 minutes, or until tender. Drain well, then set aside to cool.

2 Combine all the dressing ingredients together and season to taste with salt and pepper.

3 Cut each potato in half and place in a large bowl. Add the Bayonne ham and the celeriac, then pour the dressing over. Add the chopped herbs, reserving a pinch for the garnish, and gently mix together.

4 Just before serving, drizzle over the rapeseed oil and sprinkle with the reserved herbs.

MAKE IT *extraordinary*

Bayonne ham comes from the south-west of France, and has a slightly sweet taste.

Cornichons give a sharp-tasting crunch to the dressing.

PREP 10 MINS
COOK 25 MINS
SERVES 6

JAMES NATHAN
Champion 2008

I'm James Nathan and I won *MasterChef* in 2008. I've always wanted to be a professional chef, and since the show I've managed to work my way up to become head chef of my own kitchen at The St Enodoc Hotel in Cornwall.

What's your favourite moment from your time on the show?

It was when I was sent to Luciano for my first professional restaurant experience. It was everything I'd hoped it would be. Marco Pierre White was the owner there. The food was simple but absurdly good, and the intense pace confirmed why I loved cooking and wanted to be in a kitchen. It was basically heaven.

What was the first recipe you really made your own?

Venison with red cabbage and port is the first recipe I truly developed – it was in my meal for the final – and I still bring it onto the menu every autumn. It is all about the bounty of nature, with its deep red colours, and we serve it with deep-fried salsify, which looks like autumn leaves.

What was your worst kitchen moment?

I was with Aiden Byrne at the Dorchester, shucking huge hand-dived scallops, and I cut into them with the knife and hurt them. He was very cross. I felt upset I'd messed up, not just because he was an important chef, but because I'd hurt the beautiful scallop too.

What's your favourite kitchen tool and why?

I've had my knife so long it's become an extension of my hand. The Japanese say a knife has a soul, and have places where chefs bury their knives when they're worn out. I feel pretty close to my knife.

Who is your biggest food hero, and why?

The young Marco Pierre White when he wrote *White Heat*, my all-time favourite cookbook. The quintessential chef, he was passionate, maverick, crazy – a frenetic whirlwind of cooking fury. When I was young I used to watch chefs arguing and shouting in a kitchen from the window of my brother's flat. It turned out that the restaurant was Harvey's in Wandsworth, and the chefs I'd been watching were Gordon Ramsay and Marco!

Any advice for potential MasterChefs?

Keep things simple, allow plenty of time, and plan your cooking well. Disasters always happen, so don't panic. It's what you do when disaster strikes that sets you apart. Think quickly on your feet and incorporate the mistake as if you meant it to happen!

WALDORF SALAD WITH GRAPEFRUIT, YUZU, AND SPICED NUTS

First invented in New York in the 1890s, this salad is given a citrus-packed update with dehydrated grapefruit, yuzu mayonnaise, preserved lemon, and spiced walnuts.

1 grapefruit
pinch of sugar
500g (14oz) crisp red apples
1-2 pears
1 tbsp yuzu juice
4 celery sticks, finely diced
1 tsp finely chopped preserved lemon
25g (scant 1oz) golden sultanas
salt and freshly ground black pepper
flat-leaf parsley, to garnish

FOR THE MAYONNAISE
2 large egg yolks
1 garlic clove, finely chopped
1 tsp Dijon mustard
150ml (5fl oz) groundnut oil
125ml (4fl oz) olive oil
1 tbsp white wine vinegar
1 tsp yuzu juice

FOR THE SPICED NUTS
40g (1½oz) dark brown sugar
75g (2½oz) caster sugar
½ tsp sea salt
generous pinch of cayenne pepper
½ tsp ground cinnamon
225g (8oz) walnut halves
1 egg white

1 Prepare the dehydrated grapefruit in advance. Line a tray with lightly oiled cling film. Peel and segment the grapefruit (see p242), then arrange the segments on the tray. Sprinkle with a little sugar, then leave in a warm room for 6–12 hours.

2 Core the the apples and pears and cut them into long, thin wedges. Put them in a bowl and pour the yuzu juice over, coating the fruit well to prevent discolouring.

3 To make the mayonnaise, put the egg yolks, garlic, and mustard in a bowl. Then add half the groundnut oil, drop by drop, whisking continuously with an electric whisk. Add the vinegar to loosen the mixture. With the whisk running, add the remaining groundnut oil and the olive oil in a slow stream. When it is all incorporated, season with salt and yuzu juice to taste.

4 For the spiced nuts, preheat the oven to 150°C (300°F/ Gas 2). Mix the sugars, salt, and spices, and toss the nuts in the mixture. Whisk the egg white and 1 tbsp water until frothy but not stiff. Stir into the nut mixture. Tip onto a baking sheet lined with parchment and bake for 30 minutes, stirring occasionally to separate. Cool on a silicon mat-lined tray.

5 Take 150ml (5fl oz) of the mayonnaise (leaving the rest for another recipe), add the celery, preserved lemon, and sultanas, and season to taste with salt and pepper. Mix well, then serve, garnished with the dehydrated grapefruit, spiced nuts, and parsley.

MAKE IT
extraordinary

Dehydrating grapefruit segments intensifies their citrus flavour.

A feature of many Moroccan dishes, preserved lemon has a uniquely tart taste.

Sprinkled with cayenne and cinnamon, these walnuts add a spicy crunch to the salad.

PREP 45 MINUTES, PLUS DEHYDRATING
COOK 30 MINUTES
SERVES 4

RATATOUILLE-STUFFED COURGETTES

A more sophisticated take on the classic Provençal stew, this ratatouille is baked in courgette halves and served on a bed of fried aubergine.

5 small courgettes

5 tbsp olive oil, plus extra to serve

1 large red pepper, cut into 1cm (½in) slices

1 onion, halved and cut into 1cm (½in) slices

salt and freshly ground black pepper

2 large ripe tomatoes, cut into wedges

2 large garlic cloves, finely chopped

1 tsp finely chopped thyme leaves

½ tsp caster sugar

½ tbsp tomato purée

3 tbsp red wine

1 large aubergine, cut into 2-3mm (⅛in) thin slices

80g (2¾oz) feta cheese, crumbled

2 tbsp finely chopped flat-leaf parsley

1 Slice 4 courgettes in half lengthways and remove the seeded centres with a spoon. Blanch in salted boiling water for 4 minutes, drain, then chill in the fridge to retain their colour. Slice the remaining courgette into quarters lengthways. Cut away the seeded parts and discard. Chop the remaining flesh into approximately 1cm (½in) dice. Set aside.

2 Heat 1 tbsp of the oil in a large, heavy-based lidded frying pan. Add the red pepper, cover, and cook for 4-5 minutes over a medium heat until soft and browned in places. Set aside in a blender. Add 1 tbsp of oil to the pan and fry the onion with a pinch of salt for 2-3 minutes until softened but not browned. Add the tomatoes and cook for a further 1-2 minutes until they start to break down. Add the garlic, thyme, sugar, and tomato purée and cook until the tomato starts to catch slightly on the base of the pan. Use the wine to deglaze the pan (see p251). Add to the blender and blitz to a purée. Set aside. Preheat the oven to 200°C (400°F/Gas 6).

3 Wipe the pan clean, then add 2 tbsp of oil and return to the heat. Add the aubergine slices in a single layer (in batches, if necessary) and cook for 2-3 minutes until browned on one side. Turn and cook for a further 1-2 minutes.

4 Place the courgette halves on a lined baking sheet and fill with the purée. Sprinkle each with cheese, then bake for 8-12 minutes until heated through. Meanwhile, place a frying pan over a medium heat, add 1 tbsp oil and fry the courgette dice for 2-3 minutes until just tender. Drain on kitchen paper and keep warm. Briefly reheat the aubergine slices in the oven. To serve, arrange the aubergine slices in a circle on each plate. Carefully place 2 courgette halves on each, and scatter over the courgette dice, garnish with parsley, and drizzle with olive oil.

MAKE IT
extraordinary

Deepen the flavour of the ratatouille by adding a little full-bodied red wine to the sauce.

PREP 35 MINUTES
COOK 45 MINUTES
SERVES 4

CAULIFLOWER CHEESE CROQUETTES

Instead of a plain portion of cauliflower cheese, serve a few of these creamy, deep-fried cauliflower bites for an eye-catching side dish.

1 large cauliflower, cut into small pieces

50g (1¾oz) butter

55g (2oz) plain flour, plus extra for dredging

600ml (1 pint) whole milk

100g (3½oz) mixed grated mature Cheddar, Gruyère, and Parmesan cheeses

½ tsp grated nutmeg

1 tbsp Dijon mustard (optional)

salt and freshly ground black pepper

oil, for deep frying

1 egg, beaten

200g (7oz) panko breadcrumbs

1 Steam the cauliflower pieces until tender but still firm. Set aside.

2 Meanwhile, melt the butter in a small, heavy-based saucepan. Whisk in the flour over a low heat and cook for 2 minutes, stirring continuously. Remove from the heat and whisk in the milk, a little at a time, until smooth.

3 Return to the heat and cook, stirring continuously, for 5 minutes. Add the cheeses, nutmeg, and mustard (if using), then season and cook for 2 minutes, until the cheese has melted and the sauce is creamy.

4 Mix together the sauce and cauliflower pieces in a container. Leave to cool, then chill in the fridge for about 3 hours, or until the mixture has completely solidified.

5 Heat the oil in a deep-fat fryer or large saucepan to 180°C (350°F). Take a golf ball-sized amount of the chilled mixture and roll it into a ball. Coat it in the flour, beaten egg, and breadcrumbs. Repeat until you have used all the mixture. Carefully fry the croquettes in batches until golden, then drain on kitchen paper. Serve hot.

MAKE IT
extraordinary

A little freshly grated nutmeg enhances the flavour of the cheese sauce.

The crunchy, deep-fried panko coating contrasts with the creamy cauliflower filling.

PREP 10 MINUTES, PLUS CHILLING
COOK 35 MINUTES
SERVES 4

SLOW-COOKED SPICED RED CABBAGE WITH POMEGRANATE SEEDS

The classic foil for rich meats gets an update in this recipe. As well as tart red wine vinegar, juniper berries and star anise lend a spicy note to the cabbage, while the pomegranate seeds give a fruity pop.

50g (1¾oz) butter

25g (scant 1oz) caster sugar

1 tsp salt

90ml (3fl oz) red wine vinegar

2 star anise

20g (¾oz) fresh root ginger, peeled, and cut into thick slices

1 tsp juniper berries

1 red cabbage, about 1kg (2lb 4oz), shredded

2 tbsp redcurrant jelly

2 apples, peeled and grated

salt and freshly ground black pepper

seeds from 1 pomegranate

1 Preheat the oven to 160°C (325°F/Gas 3). Place the butter, sugar, salt, vinegar, star anise, ginger, and juniper berries in a large flameproof casserole. Add 100ml (3½fl oz) water and bring to the boil. Reduce to a simmer and cook for just 2 minutes.

2 Add the red cabbage and stir thoroughly. Seal the casserole by placing a thick piece of foil on top, followed by the lid.

3 Cook in the centre of the oven for 1½ hours. Remove the lid and foil and stir in the redcurrant jelly and apples, adding a little more water if the cabbage looks dry. Season generously, cover again, and return to the oven for a final 30 minutes.

4 Remove the star anise and ginger from the cabbage, then serve, scattered with the pomegranate seeds.

MAKE IT *extraordinary*

SIDE DISHES

As it slow-cooks, the cabbage takes on the star anise's warming, liquorice-like flavour.

Dried juniper berries add an aromatic note to the cabbage.

Sweeten the cabbage and boost its vivid colour by adding some redcurrant jelly.

PREP 20 MINUTES
COOK 2 HOURS
SERVES 4–6

MANGO AND LIME
COLESLAW

For an alternative to traditional, mayonnaise-heavy coleslaw, this colourful and fruity side includes slices of mango alongside the usual cabbage and carrot, and is tossed in a lime and chilli dressing.

3 tbsp vegetable oil

juice of 2 limes (approximately 2 tbsp)

2 tbsp palm sugar, or unrefined soft brown sugar

2–3 tbsp fish sauce

2 small bird's-eye chillies, finely chopped

3 green, unripe mangoes, peeled and sliced into long strips

1 carrot, shredded

2 spring onions, finely sliced

¼ white cabbage, shredded (about 150g/5½oz)

1 Make the dressing. In a bowl, mix together the oil, lime juice, sugar, fish sauce, and chillies, until well combined. Adjust the quantities to suit your preference – it should taste sweet, sour, salty, and hot.

2 Add the mango, carrot, spring onion, and cabbage. Mix to combine thoroughly, then serve.

Freshly squeezed lime juice adds a sharp tang to the coleslaw dressing.

The unripe mangoes' sourness balances the heat of the dressing.

PREP 10 MINUTES
SERVES 4-6

CUMIN AND CHILLI SAUTÉED BRUSSELS SPROUT LEAVES

Banish boring Brussels sprouts by frying them with toasted cumin, coriander seeds, and chilli. For a full spiced Christmas dinner, pair this recipe with those on p88, p174, and p176.

pair this recipe with those on p88, p174, and p176.

MAKE IT
extraordinary

Green chilli adds a gentle heat to the sprout leaves.

400g (14oz) Brussels sprouts, washed

1 tsp cumin seeds

1 tsp ghee or clarified butter

2 banana shallots, finely sliced

2 garlic cloves, crushed

2 green chillies, deseeded and finely chopped

thumb-sized piece of fresh root ginger, grated

½ tsp coriander seeds, crushed

25g (scant 1oz) butter

25g (scant 1oz) double cream

1 Separate the sprout leaves by slicing off their bases. Set aside.

2 Toast the cumin seeds in a dry pan, then grind in a pestle and mortar. Add the ghee to the pan, followed by the ground cumin, shallots, garlic, chilli, ginger, and coriander seeds. Fry gently until the shallots are soft. Add the butter and cream and stir until melted.

3 Add the sprout leaves and sauté in the mixture until just tender. Serve immediately.

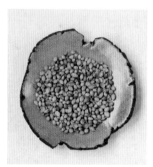

Freshly crushed coriander seeds provide a much stronger, nuttier flavour than pre-ground coriander.

PREP 15 MINUTES
COOK 10 MINUTES
SERVES 4

CARAMELIZED CARROT AND CUMIN PURÉE

While this sweet–spicy update on a simple carrot side dish is designed to go along with my Brussels sprout leaves (p172) and roast potatoes (p176) and accompany my Christmas turkey (p88), this dish will make a flavourful partner to many roast dishes.

Toast the cumin seeds to make the most of their warming, aromatic flavour.

½ tsp freshly ground cumin seeds

1.1kg (2½lb) carrots, peeled, trimmed, and halved lengthways

50g (1¾oz) butter

sprinkling of demerara sugar

1 ball stem ginger, grated

1 tsp stem ginger syrup

1 litre (1¾ pints) chicken stock

salt and freshly ground black pepper

1 In a large saucepan, briefly dry fry the cumin over a gentle heat. Add the carrots, butter, sugar, stem ginger, and ginger syrup, and cook over a medium heat for about 4 minutes, until the sugar and syrup start to caramelize.

2 Add the stock and bring to the boil, then reduce the heat and simmer for about 30 minutes, until nearly all the liquid has evaporated and the carrots are very tender. Add a little water to the pan to continue cooking if the liquid evaporates before the carrots are soft.

3 Transfer the carrot mixture to a blender. Blitz at a high speed, adding a little warm water as required, until the carrots are a smooth purée. Taste and adjust seasoning as required before serving.

Along with its syrup, stem ginger imparts a hot, sweet taste to the carrots.

PREP 10 MINUTES
COOK 45 MINUTES
SERVES 4

SPICED ROAST POTATOES

Poached in goose fat and seasoned with cumin, garam masala, and cayenne before roasting, these potatoes are crisp and spicy on the outside and perfectly fluffly on the inside. Pair them with my Christmas turkey (p88) and the sides on p172 and p174 for a full festive feast.

SIDES DISHES

MAKE IT
extraordinary

Poach the potatoes in hot goose fat to achieve crisp, golden edges.

8-12 large white potatoes, such as Desiree or Maris Piper, peeled

500-700g (1lb 2oz-1½lb) goose or duck fat

1 tsp ground cumin

1 tsp garam masala

¼ tsp cayenne pepper

pinch of salt

1 Carefully cut the potatoes into 4cm- (1¾in-) thick slices. Using an 8cm (3in) round pastry cutter, cut out a circular disc of potato from each slice.

2 Place the goose or duck fat in a heavy-based pan large enough for the potatoes to sit in one layer. Heat gently over a low heat to about 90°C (194°F). Carefully place the potatoes in the fat, ensuring they are all submerged (add more fat to cover if required). Poach in the fat for 40-50 minutes, until they are soft. Depending on the size of your pan, you may need to do this in batches, reusing the fat for each batch.

3 Meanwhile, combine the spices and salt in a small bowl. Preheat the oven to 200°C (400°F/Gas 6).

4 When the potatoes are tender, remove from the fat with a slotted spoon and place them, well spaced, in a large roasting pan. Allow a good coating of fat to remain on the potatoes. Sprinkle generously with the spice mix and spoon over a little more fat to coat them. Roast in the oven for 25-35 minutes, until crisp, turning once.

A blend of cumin, cayenne, and garam masala gives the roast potatoes a spicy coating.

PREP 20 MINUTES
COOK 1 HOUR 30 MINUTES
SERVES 4

DESSERTS AND BAKING

SPICED BLACKBERRY AND APPLE PIE WITH A CHARCOAL CRUST

The classic autumnal pie receives a dramatic makeover in this recipe, with a cardamom-spiced filling and a crust dyed jet black with activated charcoal.

215g (7½oz) plain flour, plus extra for dusting

3½ tbsp caster sugar

25g (scant 1oz) activated charcoal

¼ tsp salt

45g (1½oz) lard or white vegetable fat, chilled and cut into cubes

60g (2oz) unsalted butter, chilled and cut into cubes

FOR THE FILLING

875g (1lb 15oz) Granny Smith apples, peeled, cored, and cut into cubes

juice of 1 lemon

120g (4½oz) caster sugar, or to taste

500g (1lb 2oz) blackberries

¼ tsp ground cardamom

1 Sift the flour, 1½ tbsp sugar, charcoal, and salt into a bowl. Add the lard (or vegetable fat) and butter, and rub in with your fingers to form crumbs. Mix in water a tablespoon at a time, stopping as soon as clumps form. Press the pastry lightly into a ball, wrap in cling film, and chill in the fridge for 30 minutes.

2 Prepare the filling. Put the apples in a bowl, add the lemon juice and sugar, and toss together. Add the blackberries and cardamom and toss everything together again.

3 Preheat the oven to 190°C (375°F/Gas 5). Roll out the dough on a floured surface. Cut off a 2cm (¾in) strip that will reach around the rim of a 1-litre (1¾-pint) pie dish. Roll the rest out until it is 7.5cm (3in) larger than the dish. Place a pie funnel or upturned ovenproof cup in the dish. Spoon the fruit in around it.

4 Moisten the rim of the dish with water and place the strip of pastry on top. Brush the strip with water and place the remaining pastry over the top of the pie, then seal the edges with your finger and thumb. Chill for 15 minutes, then bake for 50-60 minutes. Sprinkle with the remaining sugar before serving.

MAKE IT
extraordinary

Edible activated charcoal is said to offer several health benefits, including aiding digestion.

Cardamom's aromatic flavour profile gives the fruit filling a gentle warmth.

PREP 20 MINUTES, PLUS CHILLING
COOK 1 HOUR
SERVES 4-6

STICKY TOFFEE PUDDING WITH DATE ICE CREAM AND RUM CARAMEL

Celebrate the best features of a sticky toffee pudding with this dessert, with a homemade ice cream full of date pieces and a rich, rum-soaked caramel sauce.

MAKE IT *extraordinary*

Give the caramel sauce an extra kick with the addition of dark rum.

110g (4oz) unsalted butter, plus extra for greasing
125g (4½oz) golden caster sugar
6 tbsp golden syrup
2 eggs
125g (4½oz) plain flour
1 tsp baking powder
pinch of salt
1 tsp vanilla paste

FOR THE ICE CREAM
500ml (16fl oz) double cream
250ml (9fl oz) whole milk
1 tbsp vanilla paste
250g (9oz) pitted dates, chopped into 5mm (¼in) pieces
6 egg yolks
150g (5½oz) caster sugar

FOR THE SAUCE
250g (9oz) caster sugar
50g (1¾oz) butter
150ml (5fl oz) double cream
1½ tbsp dark rum

1 To make the ice cream, place the cream, milk, vanilla paste, and dates into a large saucepan and bring to the boil. Remove from the heat and leave to infuse for 1 hour. Return to the heat and bring up to a simmer. In a bowl, whisk the egg yolks and sugar until pale and fluffy. Slowly add the cream mixture, while whisking to combine, then return to the pan and cook over a gentle heat, stirring continuously, until it reaches 80°C (175°F). Remove from the heat and allow to cool. Churn in an ice-cream maker according to the manufacturer's instructions, then freeze until ready to serve.

2 Grease 6 mini pudding moulds with butter. Line the bottom of each with a circle of baking parchment, then drizzle in 1 tbsp of golden syrup. Cream the sugar and butter in a bowl until pale and fluffy. Whisk in the eggs, followed by the vanilla paste, then fold in the flour, baking powder, and salt until smooth. Spoon into the moulds. Place another circle of parchment on top of each pudding, and cover with pleated foil to allow room for them to rise. Secure with string. Place the puddings in a large saucepan, and fill the pan with boiling water to three-quarters of the way up the moulds. Bring back to the boil, then simmer for 45 minutes, or until a skewer inserted through the foil comes out clean.

3 Make the sauce. Heat the sugar, butter, and 75ml (2½fl oz) water in a non-stick pan over a medium heat until the sugar dissolves. Do not stir. When it turns golden brown and starts to smell of caramel, swirl the mixture and remove from the heat. Add the cream and rum and whisk until smooth. Return to a low heat for 1 minute. Serve the puddings with a scoop of ice cream on the side and the sauce poured over.

PREP 1 HOUR, PLUS INFUSING AND FREEZING
COOK 1 HOUR 10 MINUTES
SERVES 6

FRUIT CRUMBLE WITH AMARETTO

Deepen the flavour of the autumnal medley of fruits in this crumble with the addition of bittersweet amaretto liqueur. Crushed Amaretti biscuits tossed through the topping mixture add extra texture and further bring out the almond taste.

Crushed amaretti biscuits give the crumble topping a distinctive almond flavour.

250g (9oz) sweet dessert apples, such as Cox's Orange Pippins, peeled, cored, and thinly sliced

125g (4½oz) pears, peeled, cored, and thinly sliced

125g (4½oz) blackberries

1 tbsp lemon juice

50ml (1½fl oz) amaretto liqueur

FOR THE CRUMBLE

115g (4oz) plain flour

75g (2½oz) butter

60g (2oz) rolled oats

100g (3½oz) amaretti biscuits, crushed

75g (2½oz) demerara sugar

1 Preheat the oven to 190°C (375°F/Gas 5). Put all the fruit in an ovenproof dish with the lemon juice and amaretto, and toss until well coated, to prevent the apples and pears from discolouring. Set aside.

2 To make the crumble topping, combine the flour and butter in a bowl, and rub together with your fingers until the mixture resembles coarse breadcrumbs. Stir in the oats, biscuits, and sugar.

3 Spoon the crumble mixture on top of the apples, press down gently to level the top, and bake for 45 minutes, until golden and crisp. Serve hot.

Amaretto liqueur enriches the fruit filling and complements the flavour of the biscuit topping.

PREP 10 MINUTES
COOK 45 MINUTES
SERVES 4

HONEY AND GINGER POACHED PEARS WITH MARSALA CREAM

This dessert is inspired by a Chinese recipe called double-boiled pear soup, a dish often made to help soothe a bad cough. The pears are poached in almond milk infused with honey and ginger, and paired with a rich Marsala wine whipped cream.

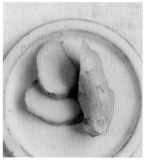

Fresh ginger adds a mellow heat to the sweet poaching liquid.

4 firm pears
200ml (7fl oz) unsweetened almond milk
150ml (5fl oz) honey
2.5cm (1in) piece of peeled fresh root ginger
1 tsp almond extract

FOR THE CREAM
230ml (8fl oz) whipping cream
1 tbsp icing sugar
60ml (2fl oz) Marsala wine

1 Peel the pears, leaving the stalks attached, and cut in half lengthways. Remove the cores with a teaspoon.

2 Place the almond milk, honey, ginger, and almond extract in a saucepan and heat gently, stirring until the honey dissolves. Add the pears, cover the pan, and simmer gently for 20 minutes, or until the pears are tender, basting frequently.

3 Remove the pears and set aside in a bowl. Remove the ginger and discard. Return the pan to the heat and boil rapidly until the liquid becomes syrupy and reduces by about one-third. Pour the reduced syrup over the pears and chill in the fridge until ready to serve.

4 In a bowl, whip the cream with the icing sugar to form soft peaks that hold their shape when you lift up the whisk. Stir in the Marsala and chill in the fridge until ready to serve.

5 Serve the pears cold with a drizzle of syrup and a generous dollop of Marsala cream.

Marsala, a fortified Italian wine, enriches the cream and goes well with the sweet pears.

PREP 15 MINUTES, PLUS CHILLING
COOK 30 MINUTES
SERVES 4

NATALIE COLEMAN MasterChef Champion 2013

SUMMER FRUIT CUP TRIFLE CAKES

Combining the quintessential tastes of a British summer, these summer trifles feature a fruit cup-flavoured jelly, orange sponge, homemade custard, and plenty of fruit.

Pimm's is designed to pair well with fresh fruit, making it perfect in a summer trifle.

FOR THE SPONGE
3 eggs
100g (3½oz) caster sugar
75g (2½oz) plain flour
1 tsp baking powder
zest of ½ orange

FOR THE JELLY
150ml (5fl oz) apple juice
150ml (5fl oz) fruit cup, such as Pimm's No. 1
zest of ½ orange
zest of ½ lemon
3 gelatine leaves, soaked in water (see p248)
16 raspberries, halved
8 strawberries, quartered

FOR THE CUSTARD
300ml (10fl oz) double cream
4 egg yolks
75g (2½oz) caster sugar
3 gelatine leaves, soaked in water (see p248)

FOR THE CREAM
200ml (7fl oz) double cream
2 tbsp icing sugar
1 tbsp orange blossom water (or to taste)

TO SERVE
grated orange zest
freeze-dried raspberries, finely chopped
a few leaves of mint

1 Make the sponge. Preheat the oven to 180°C (350°F/Gas 4) and line a Swiss roll tin with baking parchment. Beat the eggs and sugar in a bowl until pale and fluffy, then sift in the flour and baking powder. Fold in the orange zest and mix until well combined. Pour the mixture into the lined tin and spread out evenly. Bake for 12 minutes, until set, then remove from the oven and allow to cool. Remove the sponge from the tin and cut out 4 circles using 10cm (4in) presentation moulds. Grease the moulds and place a sponge inside each. Wrap the bottom of each mould with cling film and place on a lined baking tray.

2 Make the jelly. Combine the apple juice, fruit cup, and orange and lemon zest in a saucepan and heat until hot but not boiling. Squeeze out the gelatine and whisk it into the mixture until combined. Leave to cool slightly. Divide the berries between the moulds, then pour one-quarter of the jelly mixture into each. Refrigerate for 1 hour, or until set.

3 To make the custard, whisk the egg yolks and sugar together until pale and fluffy. Bring the double cream to boiling point in a pan, then gradually pour it over the egg yolks and sugar, stirring to combine. Return the mixture to the pan and heat gently until it reaches 80°C (175°F), then transfer to a bowl. Allow to cool slightly, then whisk in the drained gelatine. Divide between the moulds and return them to the fridge for about 3 hours, or until completely set.

4 Whisk the cream, icing sugar, and orange blossom water until stiff peaks form. Remove the cling film and unmould the trifles onto plates. Pipe peaks of cream onto each trifle and garnish with the orange zest, raspberries, and mint to serve.

Zested orange peel features in several components, lending a citrus note overall.

Along with the zest and mint, freeze-dried raspberries add a vibrant pop of colour to the dish.

PREP 45 MINUTES
COOK 30 MINUTES, PLUS CHILLING
SERVES 4

BLACKBERRY TARTLETS WITH LAVENDER ICE CREAM

Instead of the usual crème pâtissière filling, these hot tartlets are topped with floral lavender ice cream. This dessert can be prepared in advance up to step 3.

The tartness of the fresh blackberries cuts through the smooth lavender ice cream.

FOR THE ICE CREAM
150ml (5fl oz) double cream
3 tbsp milk
2 eggs, plus 2 egg yolks
50g (1¾oz) caster sugar
10 drops of cold lavender extract

FOR THE HONEYCOMB
5 tbsp sugar
2 tbsp golden syrup
1 tsp bicarbonate of soda

FOR THE PASTRY
175g (6oz) plain flour, plus extra for dusting
30g (1oz) caster sugar
100g (3½oz) unsalted butter, chilled and diced
1 egg, beaten with 1 tbsp iced water

FOR THE TOPPING
6 tbsp apricot jam, sieved
250g (9oz) blackberries

1 Make the ice cream a day in advance. Heat the milk and cream in a small, heavy-based saucepan until hot but not boiling. In a heatproof bowl, whisk the eggs, egg yolks, sugar, and lavender extract. Gradually stir in the hot milk to make a custard. Churn in an ice-cream maker according to manufacturer's instructions.

2 Make the honeycomb. Heat the sugar and syrup over a low heat for 2 minutes, stirring constantly. Take care not to let it burn. Stir in the bicarbonate of soda, then immediately pour the foaming mixture onto a silicone sheet and leave to cool. Once cooled, place the honeycomb in a plastic bag and tap with a rolling pin to crush it. Set aside at room temperature, sealed in the bag.

3 Prepare sweet shortcrust pastry using the flour, caster sugar, butter, and egg mixture (see p247), and chill for 30 minutes. Preheat the oven to 180°C (350°F/Gas 4). Divide the pastry into 4 portions. On a lightly floured surface, roll out each portion to a circle 3mm (⅛in) thick, and use to line four 10cm (4in) tartlet cases, leaving an overhang of at least 1cm (½in). Prick the tartlet bases and blind bake for 15 minutes (see p247), then remove the beans and bake for another 5–10 minutes, until crisp. Trim the pastry overhang with a sharp knife, then leave them to cool completely in their tins before turning them out.

4 To serve, heat the jam and 1 tbsp water in a pan over a low heat, stirring until smooth. Fill each tart case with the blackberries, then brush with the apricot glaze. Return the filled tarts to the oven for 5 minutes, then serve hot, topped with a quenelle of the ice cream and sprinkled with honeycomb.

Store honeycomb in a sealed bag in a cool, dry place before using to keep it crunchy.

PREP 35 MINUTES, PLUS CHILLING
COOK 50 MINUTES, PLUS FREEZING
SERVES 4

ANGELLICA BELL
Celebrity Champion 2017

I have always enjoyed food, so teaching myself to cook was a natural progression. I get so much pleasure cooking for others, especially desserts. Anything I create to has to look fantastic on the plate, which makes sense because, before anything else, we eat with our eyes!

What's your favourite moment from your time on the show, and why?

Being on *Celebrity MasterChef* was one big rollercoaster. There were times when I wasn't sure if I could handle the pressure but, somehow, I kept moving forward in the competition. The high point had to be cooking in the kitchen of Jason Atherton's restaurant, City Social. I was given the task of replicating his chocolate and olive oil dessert, and then had to serve it to Marcus Wareing, Atul Kochhar, Nieves Barragan Mohacho, Lisa Goodwin-Allen, and Alyn Williams – all Michelin-star cooking heavyweights who are at the top of their game. It was an incredible day – I'll never forget it.

What was the first recipe you really made your own?

For me, the recipe I really made my own was the Baked Alaska which I cooked for John and Gregg. I spent so much time thinking about the elements I wanted to produce, as well as the flavours that would complement each other. It was quite an emotional day as all our dishes had to be dedicated to someone we loved – what I chose to do was technically challenging, especially in the time allocated, so I wasn't sure if I could pull it off. I'm not quite sure how I managed it, but I'm so relieved I did!

What was your worst kitchen moment?

Most people remember me burning milk in my first appearance on the show. I do put some of the blame on Gregg though, as I was struggling to use the induction hob and he wanted to have a full-on chat. He's great and thought it was hilarious. I still can't believe my milk boiled over on national television!

What's your favourite ingredient, and why?

One of my favourite ingredients is cinnamon. I love it in everything – porridge, pancakes, cinnamon buns, cinnamon toast, stewed apples, tea – you name it, I'll try and get some cinnamon in it.

Who's your biggest food hero, and why?

My food hero is my grandmother who, when I was younger, spent most of her time in the kitchen cooking for her family or anyone who walked through her door. She taught me the basics of cooking, knife skills, and generally to love food and eating. She's 98 now and barely recognises me but I'll always be eternally grateful to her for setting me off on my culinary journey.

PEAR, PASSIONFRUIT, AND RASPBERRY PAVLOVA

This double-layered pavlova combines poached pears, macerated raspberries, two types of cream, and toasted pistachios to make an unashamedly decadent dessert.

6 egg whites, at room
temperature
pinch of salt
350g (12oz) caster sugar
2 tsp cornflour
2 tsp white vinegar
200g (8oz) shelled pistachios

FOR THE PEARS
500g (1lb 2oz) passionfruit
purée
3 tbsp pear liqueur
100g (3½oz) granulated sugar
6 pears, peeled but retaining
stalks
pulp of 6 passionfruits

FOR THE RASPBERRIES
500g (1lb 2oz) raspberries
4 tbsp icing sugar
90-120ml (3-4fl oz) balsamic
vinegar

**FOR THE MARSCAPONE
CREAM**
250g (9oz) mascarpone
200g (7oz) natural fromage frais
1 tsp vanilla extract
1-2 tbsp caster sugar
milk, to loosen

**FOR THE WHITE CHOCOLATE
CREAM**
100g (4oz) white chocolate,
broken into small pieces
530ml (19fl oz) double cream

1 Preheat the oven to 130°C (250°F/Gas ½). Draw two 20cm (8in) circles on greaseproof paper and place on baking trays. Make the meringue (see p249), whisking in the cornflour and vinegar once the mixture is glossy and firm. Spoon into the circles and bake for 1½ hours, then turn off the oven, leaving the meringues inside until cool.

2 Combine the passionfruit purée, liqueur, sugar, and 300ml (10fl oz) water in a large pan. Add the pears and simmer over a medium heat for about 30 minutes, until soft and tender. Remove the pears and stand them upright on a plate to cool, then refrigerate. Continue to simmer the poaching liquid until it reduces to a thick syrup. Let it cool. Discard half of the syrup. Stir the passionfruit pulp through the remaining syrup. Set aside.

3 Combine the raspberries, icing sugar, and balsamic vinegar in a bowl, and leave to macerate for 30-40 minutes. In another bowl, whisk together the mascarpone, fromage frais, vanilla, and sugar in a bowl until smooth, adding a dash of milk to loosen if necessary. Cover and chill until needed.

4 Preheat the oven to 180°C (350°F/Gas 4). Heat the chocolate and 60ml (2fl oz) cream in a pan, stirring occasionally, until melted and combined. Leave to cool. Beat the remaining cream to soft peaks in a bowl, then gently fold in the cooled chocolate mixture and refrigerate.

5 Bake the pistachios on a tray for 6-8 minutes. Rub in a clean tea towel to remove the skins. Leave to cool, then chop.

6 Spread the mascarpone cream over one meringue, followed by the raspberries and half of the pistachios. Top with the second meringue and cover with the white chocolate cream. Stand the pears on top, drizzle with passionfruit syrup, sprinkle with the remaining pistachios, and serve.

MAKE IT *extraordinary*

The intense, nutty flavour of toasted pistachios contrasts with the sweetness of the pavlova.

Intensify the sweetness of the raspberries by macerating them with balsamic vinegar.

Top the pavlova with a layer of whipped cream enriched with white chocolate ganache.

PREP 1 HOUR
COOK 1 HOUR 30 MINUTES,
PLUS COOLING
SERVES 12

SANSHO LEMON SORBET

Made with just four ingredients, this unusual lemon sorbet nonetheless packs quite a kick. The addition of Japanese sansho pepper to the syrup mixture produces a light tingling sensation with every mouthful, to match the tart taste of the lemon.

Sansho pepper tastes a little like ginger and lemongrass, making it ideal for pairing with citrus.

6 large unwaxed lemons
250g (9oz) sugar
1 tbsp Japanese sansho pepper, plus extra to garnish
1 large egg white

1 Use a vegetable peeler to remove thin strips of peel from 3 of the lemons (see p242). Make sure you don't include any white pith, or the sorbet will be bitter. Put the sugar, lemon peel, sansho pepper, and 250ml (9fl oz) water in a pan and bring to the boil. Boil for 5 minutes to make a syrup. Remove from the heat and allow to cool.

2 Squeeze the juice from all of the lemons and pour into a measuring jug. Add enough water to make the juice up to 400ml (14fl oz). Mix with the cooled syrup, then cover and chill in the fridge overnight.

3 Pour the mixture into a container, cover, and freeze for 1–2 hours, or until about 2.5cm (1in) of the mixture is frozen around the sides. Whisk to break up the ice particles, then cover and return to the freezer. After another 30 minutes, whisk again until smooth, then fold in the lightly beaten egg white. Continue freezing the sorbet until firm.

4 Transfer the sorbet to the fridge about 30 minutes before serving, to allow it to soften slightly. Serve in scoops, garnished with freshly ground sansho pepper.

ALTERNATIVELY, if you have an ice-cream maker, strain the mixture into the bowl and follow the instructions for freezing. When the sorbet mixture starts to look icy, lightly beat the egg white to loosen it, and add to the mixture. When the sorbet is firm, transfer it to the freezer until 30 minutes before serving, then continue with step 4.

PREP 30 MINUTES, PLUS CHILLING AND FREEZING
MAKES 750ML (1¼ PINTS)

COFFEE AND CHOCOLATE FONDANT WITH WALNUT ICE CREAM

Inspired by the classic flavours of coffee and walnut cake, this espresso-infused hot chocolate fondant finds a perfect partner in the nutty homemade ice cream.

FOR THE ICE CREAM
500ml (16fl oz) double cream

250ml (9fl oz) whole milk

1 tsp walnut essence

6 egg yolks

150g (5½oz) caster sugar

200g (7oz) shelled walnuts, finely chopped, plus extra to serve

FOR THE FONDANT
1 tbsp cocoa powder

125g (4½oz) dark chocolate, 70 per cent cocoa

125g (4½oz) unsalted butter, plus extra for greasing

2 eggs, plus 2 egg yolks

100g (3½oz) caster sugar

4 tbsp espresso coffee

3 tbsp plain flour

1 coffee bean, grated, for garnish

1 Prepare the ice cream. Combine the double cream, milk, and walnut essence in a large saucepan and bring to the boil. Remove from the heat and leave to infuse for 1 hour. Return to the heat and bring up to a simmer.

2 Combine the egg yolks and sugar in a bowl, and whisk until pale and fluffy. Slowly add the cream mixture to the bowl, whisking to combine, then return to the pan and heat gently, constantly stirring with a spatula, until it reaches 80°C (175°F). Remove from the heat and allow to cool.

3 Transfer the mixture to an ice-cream maker. Gradually add the walnut pieces while churning for 45 minutes, or until it reaches the right consistency. Freeze until ready to serve.

4 Make the fondants. Preheat the oven to 180°C (350°F/Gas 4). Grease 4 mini pudding moulds with butter, then dust with cocoa powder.

5 Carefully melt the chocolate and butter in a heatproof bowl over a pan of gently simmering water, then remove from the heat and leave for 5 minutes to cool slightly. While it cools, whisk together the eggs, egg yolks, and sugar until pale and fluffy. Mix in the chocolate mixture and the coffee, then fold in sift in the flour and fold in gently to incoporate. Divide the mixture between the pudding moulds and bake in the oven for 12 minutes, or until the top has set. Remove from the oven and leave to stand for 1 minute.

6 Transfer the fondants to plates. Serve with the walnuts, a quenelle of ice cream, and a grating of coffee bean.

MAKE IT *extraordinary*

Walnuts add a crunch that contrasts with the molten fondant centres.

Finish the dish with a grating of espresso bean to accentuate the flavour of the fondant.

PREP 15 MINUTES, PLUS INFUSING AND FREEZING
COOK 30 MINUTES
SERVES 4

CASSIA, CARDAMOM, AND ROSEWATER RICE PUDDING

Easily transform this classic pudding into something a little more extravagant with the addition of a few spices, a splash of rosewater, and a scattering of crunchy flaked almonds. Top with gold leaf and edible rose petals for a truly luxurious touch.

MAKE IT
extraordinary

Like cinnamon, cassia is a warm, sweet spice, but its flavour is a little more pungent.

15g (½oz) butter, plus extra for greasing

60g (2oz) short-grain rice, such as Arborio

600ml (1 pint) full-fat milk

20g (¾oz) sultanas

1 cassia stick or cinnamon stick

10 green cardamom pods

30g (1oz) caster sugar

2 tsp rosewater

20g (¾oz) flaked almonds

edible rose petals, to garnish (optional)

1-2 sheets of gold leaf, to garnish (optional)

1 Lightly grease a large baking dish with butter. Rinse the rice under cold running water, then drain well. Pour the rice, milk, sultanas, cassia, and cardamom pods into the dish, and leave to rest for 30 minutes.

2 Preheat the oven to 150°C (300°F/Gas 2). Add the sugar to the pudding, stir, then dot with the butter. Bake for 2-2½ hours, or until the skin of the pudding is golden. Just before serving, stir though the rosewater. Garnish each portion with flaked almonds, rose petals, and gold leaf, if using.

Whole cardamom pods enrich the pudding with their sweet-spicy flavour.

PREP 10 MINUTES, PLUS RESTING
COOK 2 HOURS 30 MINUTES
SERVES 4

BRULÉED LIME AND CHOCOLATE TART

Turn the classic tarte au citron on its head with this recipe, which substitutes lemon for lime and is baked in a rich chocolate shortcrust pastry case. The brulée topping adds a final touch of caramelization.

Candied lime peel strips garnish the tart, highlighting the flavour of the filling.

FOR THE CANDIED LIME PEEL

peel of 3 limes, white pith removed

100g (3½oz) caster sugar, plus extra to coat

FOR THE PASTRY

175g (6oz) plain flour, plus extra for dusting

2 tbsp cocoa powder

85g (3oz) butter, chilled

45g (1½oz) caster sugar

1 egg

FOR THE FILLING

5 eggs

200g (7oz) caster sugar

zest and juice of 6 limes

250ml (9fl oz) double cream

icing sugar, for dusting

1 Slice the lime peel into fine strips. Add the strips to a pan of boiling water and cook for 1 minute, then remove with a slotted spoon and plunge into iced water. Drain the peel. In a second pan, prepare a syrup (see p248) with the sugar and 100ml (3½fl oz) water. Add the peel and cook over a medium-high heat, stirring occasionally, for 5 minutes. Remove with a slotted spoon, toss with caster sugar to coat, and leave to dry on baking parchment.

2 To make the pastry, put the flour, cocoa powder, butter, and sugar into a food processor and pulse until it resembles breadcrumbs. Lightly beat the egg with a fork, add the egg, and mix until the pastry draws together into a ball. Wrap in cling film and chill in the fridge for 30 minutes. Roll it out on a lightly floured surface and use to line the bottom and sides of a 20cm (8in) tart tin. Cover with cling film and return to the fridge for at least 30 minutes.

3 To make the filling, beat the eggs and sugar together until combined. Beat in the lime zest and juice, then whisk in the cream until everything is smooth and combined. Chill for 1 hour.

4 Preheat the oven to 190°C (375°F/Gas 5). Blind bake for 10 minutes (see p247), then remove the paper and beans, and bake for a further 5 minutes, or until the bottom is crisp. Reduce the oven temperature to 150°C (300°F/Gas 2). Place the tart tin on a baking tray and pour in the lime filling, being careful not to allow the filling to spill over the edges. Bake for 35–40 minutes, or until just set. Remove from the oven and set aside to cool. Just before serving, dust with icing sugar and lightly brulée with a blow torch. Divide into slices, garnish with candied lime zest, and serve.

PREP 35 MINUTES, PLUS CHILLING
COOK 1 HOUR
SERVES 8

VODKA, VANILLA, AND THYME PANNA COTTA WITH RHUBARB

The sharp taste of vodka and a savoury touch of thyme create a complex blend of flavours in an otherwise sweet and creamy vanilla panna cotta, while a side of oven-roasted rhubarb gives this dessert an added burst of pastel colour.

400ml (14fl oz) single cream
250ml (9fl oz) whole milk
2 fresh vanilla pods, split lengthways
4-5 sprigs of thyme
100g (3½oz) caster sugar
5 sheets of gelatine
2 tbsp vodka
1 tbsp sunflower oil
250g (9oz) fresh rhubarb, cut into 2-3cm (1in) pieces
2-3 tbsp caster sugar
100ml (3½fl oz) apple juice

1 Heat the cream and milk in a saucepan with the vanilla pods and 2 of the thyme sprigs. When it is hot, but not boiling, pour it into a bowl, and whisk in the sugar until dissolved.

2 Soak the gelatine in a bowl of water for 5 minutes, then squeeze out the excess and add to the hot cream. Return to the pan and heat the mixture very gently, stirring, until the gelatine dissolves. Stir through the vodka and remove the vanilla and thyme.

3 Rub the insides of four 150ml (5fl oz) ramekins with a piece of kitchen paper dipped in the oil. Divide the cream mixture between the ramekins, cover, and cool. Transfer to the fridge to chill for at least 2 hours, or until set.

4 Meanwhile, preheat the oven to 200°C (400°F/Gas 6). Place the rhubarb in a roasting tray, spoon over the sugar and apple juice, and cook in the oven for 10 minutes, or until soft. Leave to cool, then set aside until required.

5 When ready to serve, mash or press through a sieve 2 tablespoons of the rhubarb and use to decorate the plates. Fill a bowl with hot water and carefully dip the base of each ramekin into the water. Run a small knife around the edge of the panna cotta and turn out onto plates. Serve with the rest of the roasted rhubarb, and garnish with thyme leaves from the remaining sprigs.

MAKE IT *extraordinary*

Opt for forced rhubarb if you can - it has a delicate flavour and vivid pink colour.

Infusing the cream with thyme as well as vanilla gives the dessert a subtle herbal flavour.

A shot of vodka enriches the panna cotta without overwhelming it.

PREP 15 MINUTES
COOK 20 MINUTES, PLUS CHILLING
SERVES 4

SHELINA PERMALLOO
Champion 2012

My name is Shelina Permalloo and I won *MasterChef* in 2012. Since the show, I've written two cookbooks, appeared on TV, worked in professional kitchens, and opened my own restaurant, Lakaz Maman, in Southampton.

Q What's your favourite moment from your time on the show?

A It was when I cooked at de Karmelliat, a Michelin three-star restaurant in Bruges. The chef looked like Santa Claus.

Q What was the first recipe you really made your own?

A During *MasterChef* I cooked this soft-shell crab and it made John well up with tears. I remember him saying "you've come home". For a while I wondered what that meant, but eventually I realized I had figured out my food style and for me that was the beginning of my food journey.

Q What was your worst kitchen moment?

A My worst kitchen moment was a recent Saturday service in my new restaurant, Lakaz Maman. All the fryers went down at eight o'clock at night, and then everything went down. I later found out it was because a seagull flew into the extractor and blew the whole thing up. We had no kitchen, and had to find fryers from other places. Although we made do and it was fine, it was still the worst night of my life.

Q What's your favourite kitchen tool and why?

A I can't live without a microplane. And I wouldn't be able to live without a speed peeler – those are two things I love.

Q Best meal of the day: breakfast, lunch, or dinner?

A I don't have a structured day – that's probably the life of a chef. So it tends to be when I'm relaxed, which is when I've finished service. So, a midnight dinner?

Q Who is your biggest food hero and why?

A It would always be my mum. Everything I learnt was from her, and from my aunts, and grandmothers, and uncles, and family in Mauritius. So I think for me it's all about learning about the traditions of what it is I cook, and being a Mauritian chef.

Q Any advice for potential MasterChefs?

A The most important thing is be yourself. Just learn how to cook really delicious food and you'll learn the rest as you go along, but you also have to love what you are cooking.

PIÑA COLADA SYLLABUB WITH CANDIED PINEAPPLE

The classic lemon syllabub gets a tropical makeover with the addition of fresh pineapple and toasted coconut flakes, plus a garnish of homemade candied pineapple slices. All the fruity flavours of a piña colada cocktail, without the inevitable hangover.

MAKE IT
extraordinary

Coconut is the perfect partner for tangy pineapple, and gives the creamy syllabub extra texture.

FOR THE CANDIED PINEAPPLE

4 thin slices of fresh pineapple, skin removed

250g (9oz) caster sugar

FOR THE SYLLABUB

juice of 1 lime

4-5 tbsp caster sugar

300ml (10fl oz) double cream

50g (1³⁄₄oz) finely chopped pineapple

¹⁄₃ coconut, finely grated, toasted in a dry pan

finely grated lime zest, to decorate

1. The day before you plan to serve the syllabub, prepare the candied pineapple. Place the pineapple slices into boiling water and blanch for 1 minute, then submerge into iced water to cool. Drain.

2. Place 240ml (8fl oz) of water in a saucepan. Add 200g (7oz) of the sugar and dissolve gently over a low heat. Once the sugar has dissolved, add the pineapple slices. Do not stir, but move the pan to ensure the pineapple slices are fully immersed. Simmer for 1½ hours.

3. Remove the pineapple from the pan with a slotted spoon. Toss with the remaining 50g (1³⁄₄oz) of sugar, and leave to dry for at least 24 hours on a wire rack before using.

4. To make the syllabub, place the lime juice in a bowl, add the sugar, and stir until it starts to dissolve. Pour in the cream and whisk until the mixture forms soft peaks. Fold in the chopped pineapple and toasted coconut.

5. Spoon into 4 serving glasses, and chill in the fridge for 30 minutes. Garnish with the lime zest and a slice of candied pineapple.

Prepare the candied pineapple garnish the day before serving the syllabub.

PREP 20 MINUTES
COOK 1 HOUR 40 MINUTES, PLUS DRYING AND CHILLING
SERVES 4

BOOZY GOOSEBERRY FOOL WITH GINGER SHORTBREAD

Round out the sweet-sour taste and smooth, creamy texture of a classic gooseberry fool with elderflower liqueur and freshly baked ginger shortbread.

500g (1lb 2oz) gooseberries
20g (³/₄oz) unsalted butter
200g (7oz) sugar
small knob of fresh root ginger, peeled and cut into 2 slices
3 tbsp elderflower liqueur
300ml (10fl oz) double cream

FOR THE SHORTBREAD
80g (2³/₄fl oz) unsalted butter, plus extra for greasing
80g (2³/₄fl oz) plain flour
1 tsp ground ginger
30g (1oz) icing sugar
30g (1oz) rice flour
drop of vanilla extract

1 Top and tail the gooseberries. In a heavy-based saucepan, heat them gently in the butter, along with the sugar and ginger. Make sure the sugar and gooseberries do not catch on the surface of the pan and caramelize before they soften and produce liquid, as this will affect the flavour. Cook for 10-15 minutes, until soft.

2 Mash the cooked fruit or pass it through a coarse sieve, then leave to cool. Discard the ginger slices. Add the elderflower liqueur and mix well. Whip the cream to soft peaks, then fold in the fruit purée, reserving 4 tbsp. Taste the fruit-cream mixture to check the sweetness – it should have a tart, refreshing flavour. Spoon into serving glasses, swirl through the reserved purée, and refrigerate until needed.

3 To make the shortbread, cream the butter in a bowl until pale and fluffy. Sift in the flour, ginger, icing sugar, and rice flour, and beat well. Beat in the vanilla. Shape into a ball and wrap with cling film. Chill in the fridge for 1 hour.

4 Preheat the oven to 180°C (350°F/Gas 4). Roll out the dough on a floured surface to a thickness of 1cm (½in). Cut out the shortbreads with a cookie cutter and place them, spaced well apart, on a baking sheet lined with baking parchment. Bake for 10-15 minutes, until golden.

5 Carefully transfer the shortbreads to a wire rack to cool, then dust with icing sugar before serving alongside the fool. Garnish with shortbread crumbs.

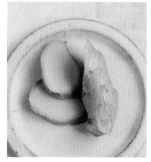

Infuse the gooseberries with fresh ginger to echo the flavour of the shortbread.

Elderflower liqueur gives the gooseberry purée a delicate floral kick.

PREP 40 MINUTES, PLUS CHILLING
COOK 30 MINUTES
SERVES 4-6

DECONSTRUCTED ETON MESS

I'm usually not a huge fan of "deconstructing" recipes, but I've made an exception with this dish: a light, fun, and colourful play on a classic summer pudding.

500ml (16fl oz) double cream

1 tsp vanilla extract

2 tbsp caster sugar

2 egg whites

100g (3½oz) golden caster sugar

250g (9oz) strawberries, cut in half lengthways

FOR THE MINT JELLY

100g (3½oz) caster sugar

4 gelatine leaves, soaked (see p248)

½ bunch of mint, leaves picked, plus extra to garnish

FOR THE STRAWBERRY GEL

250g (9oz) strawberries

100ml (3½fl oz) water

1 heaped tsp agar agar flakes

2 gelatine leaves, soaked (see p248)

FOR THE RASPBERRY COULIS

250g (9oz) raspberries

1 tbsp icing sugar

juice of ½ lemon

1 Preheat the oven to 150°C (300°F/Gas 2). Prepare the meringue (see p249), then spread a 2mm- (⅛in-) thick layer onto a non-stick silicone mat or baking parchment. Place in the oven, reduce the temperature to 120°C (250°F), and bake for 1½–2 hours, until the meringue is crisp and dry. Turn off the oven and leave inside for another hour. Remove and break into shards.

2 Meanwhile, prepare the jelly. Line a flat container with cling film. Prepare the sugar syrup using the sugar and 100ml (3½fl oz) water (see p248), then remove from the heat. Add the mint leaves and leave to infuse for 15 minutes. Stir the prepared gelatine into the syrup. If the gelatine does not fully dissolve, return the syrup to a very low heat and stir constantly until smooth. Pass through a fine sieve into the prepared container to form a 1cm- (½in-) thick layer, then refrigerate until set.

5 For the strawberry gel, blend the strawberries in a food processor until smooth, then pass through a sieve. Combine with the agar agar and 100ml (3½fl oz) water in a saucepan and bring to the boil. Leave to cool slightly, then add the soaked gelatine. Stir to combine and set aside.

6 Put all the raspberry coulis ingredients in a pan and heat until the raspberries break down. Blitz to a purée in a blender, then pass through a fine non-metallic sieve. Keep warm.

7 Remove the jelly from the container, peel off the cling film, and slice into 1cm (½in) cubes. Whisk the cream until stiff, then whisk in the vanilla extract and sugar. Pipe or spoon neat mounds of cream and strawberry gel onto each plate, add the meringue shards, mint jelly, and strawberry halves, then drizzle with coulis and garnish with mint leaves.

MAKE IT *extraordinary*

Unlike a classic Eton mess, the meringue is not mixed into the cream, keeping the shards crisp.

Fresh, fragrant cubes of mint jelly add a pop of colour and concentrated flavour to the plate.

A tangy strawberry gel, set with agar agar and gelatine, takes the dish to a professional level.

PREP 30 MINUTES, PLUS CHILLING

COOK 2 HOURS 15 MINUTES

SERVES 4

CHAI CRÈME BRÛLÉE

Cinnamon, cardamom, cloves, ginger, and two bags of Darjeeling are steeped in a rich vanilla custard mixture to infuse this classic dessert with the comforting, aromatic flavours of spiced tea.

MAKE IT
extraordinary

A blend of spices including ginger, cinnamon, and cardamom make up chai's warming flavour profile.

5 egg yolks

75g (2½oz) caster sugar, plus 4 tbsp extra for the topping

1 tsp vanilla bean paste

500ml (16fl oz) whipping cream

1 cinnamon stick

5 cloves

3 cardamon pods

½ tsp ground ginger

2 bags Darjeeling tea

1 Preheat the oven to 160°C (325°F/Gas 3). In a large bowl, whisk together the egg yolks, sugar, and vanilla. Place the cream in a saucepan with the sugar, spices, and tea bags, and infuse gently over a low heat until hot. Remove from the heat before it starts to boil. Sieve to remove the spices, then pour the cream into the egg yolk mixture, whisking constantly.

2 Place four 200ml (7fl oz) ramekins in a roasting tray. Pour the custard mixture into the ramekins. Carefully fill the roasting tray to halfway up the sides of the ramekins with hot water, being careful not to splash any into the custards. Transfer to the oven and cook for 30-40 minutes, until they are just set, but still wobbling slightly in the middle.

3 Refrigerate the custards for at least 2 hours. When ready to serve, sprinkle 1 tbsp of caster sugar over each custard and gently spread it out with the back of a teaspoon. Preheat the grill on its highest setting, or take out your blowtorch.

4 If using a grill, place the custards on a baking sheet, put them very close to a very hot grill, and watch them carefully. Remove as soon as the sugar has melted to a dark brown caramel. If using a blowtorch, sweep the flame evenly over the sugar until it melts.

PREP 25 MINUTES
COOK 45 MINUTES,
PLUS CHILLING
SERVES 4

GRANARY AND CHERRY TREACLE TART

My treacle tart gains its nutty depth of flavour from the browned butter and granary breadcrumbs, and includes a surprise layer of tart cherry jam beneath the treacle filling.

FOR THE JAM
200g (7oz) pitted Morello or black cherries

juice and finely grated zest of 1 lemon

100g (3½oz) sugar

FOR THE PASTRY
175g (6oz) plain flour, plus extra for dusting

85g (3oz) butter, cubed

1 tsp caster sugar

1 egg yolk

FOR THE FILLING
50g (1¾oz) butter

3 tbsp cream

1 egg

finely grated zest of 1 lemon

350g (12oz) golden syrup

100g (3½oz) breadcrumbs, made from a Granary loaf

1 Make the jam by placing the ingredients in a heavy-based saucepan. Simmer over a low heat for 20 minutes. For the last 5 minutes, stir regularly to prevent the jam catching and burning. Remove from the heat and allow to cool slightly.

2 Preheat the oven to 160°C (375°F/Gas 5). To make the pastry, sift the flour into a bowl. Add the butter, and rub in with fingertips until the mixture resembles coarse breadcrumbs. Add the sugar. Mix the egg yolk with 3 tbsp cold water, and pour into the mixture. Combine to form a dough.

3 On a lightly floured surface, roll the pastry into a circle large enough to line a 20cm (8in) round tart tin, allowing the pastry to extend over the edges. Prick the pastry lightly all over with a fork. Chill in the fridge for 30 minutes.

4 Bake the pastry case in the oven for 10 minutes until just starting to colour. Remove from the oven and spread with a thin layer of cherry jam. Leave to cool completely.

5 To make the filling, melt the butter in a heavy-based pan over a low heat until foaming and starting to brown. Remove from the heat, immediately add the cream, and whisk until it cools. Add the egg, lemon zest, and golden syrup, and whisk to combine. Add the breadcrumbs and mix well, then pour the filling into the tart base.

6 Bake in the oven for 25–30 minutes. Remove from the oven and trim the pastry edges with a knife. Leave to cool for about 10 minutes before serving.

MAKE IT *extraordinary*

Homemade cherry jam gives the tart a sharp tang to balance out the sweet filling.

Granary breadcrumbs give the treacle filling some bite, as well as a deep, malty flavour.

PREP 20 MINUTES, PLUS CHILLING
COOK 1 HOUR
SERVES 8

IRISH CREAM BREAD AND BUTTER PUDDING

Smooth-tasting Irish cream liqueur makes the perfect addition to the custard base of a classic bread and butter pudding. Paired with the anise flavours of fennel seed and Pernod-soaked sultanas, this is a sophisticated twist on a classic comfort-food dessert.

Plump up and enrich the sultanas by soaking them in an anise-flavoured liqueur.

The croissants' many layers absorb the custard easily.

- 50g (1¾oz) sultanas
- 3 tbsp anise-flavoured liqueur, such as Pernod
- 40g (1¼oz) butter, softened, plus extra for greasing
- 3 slices of day-old white bread, crusts cut off
- 2 croissants
- 350ml (12fl oz) whole milk
- 200ml (7fl oz) Irish cream liqueur, such as Baileys
- 2 eggs, lightly beaten
- ½ tsp ground cinnamon
- finely grated zest of 1 lemon
- ½ tsp ground fennel seed
- 3 tbsp caster sugar
- vanilla custard, to serve

1 Combine the sultanas and anise-flavoured liqueur in a bowl. Leave to soak for 10 minutes.

2 Grease a medium ovenproof dish. Butter the bread and cut each slice into 4 triangles. Cut the croissants into similar-sized slices.

3 Arrange half the bread and croissant slices in the base of the dish. Sprinkle over half the sultanas. Top with the remaining bread and croissants, in neat rows, and then sprinkle over the remaining sultanas.

4 Preheat the oven to 180°C (350°F/Gas 4). Combine the milk, Irish cream liqueur, eggs, cinnamon, lemon zest, ground fennel seed, and 2 tbsp of the sugar in a jug, and whisk with a fork until well combined. Pour the mixture over the bread. Set aside for at least 15 minutes to allow the custard to soak into the bread. Push the sultanas under the custard so they don't burn in the oven.

5 Sprinkle the remaining sugar over the top of the pudding and bake in the oven for 25–35 minutes, or until golden brown. Remove from the oven and set aside for 10–15 minutes. Serve warm, with vanilla custard.

PREP 20 MINUTES, PLUS RESTING
COOK 35 MINUTES
SERVES 4

BRAMBLE AND ROSE AUTUMN PUDDING

This twist on the classic summer pudding uses autumn's hedgerow harvest to create a dark and delicious dessert. Rosewater complements the berries well, but make sure not to use too much, or the floral taste will overpower the other flavours.

The sticky juices from the fresh, seasonal berries dye the bread a vivid red–purple colour.

10 slices of white bread, crusts removed

300g (10oz) blueberries

150g (5½oz) caster sugar

juice and finely grated zest of 1 lemon

400g (14oz) blackberries

1–2 tsp rosewater

1 Line a 1 litre (1¾ pint) pudding basin with cling film. Cut out a circle of bread to fit the base, then overlap the remaining bread slices evenly around the sides of the basin.

2 Cook 200g (7oz) of the blueberries with the sugar, lemon juice, and zest over a low heat for about 10 minutes, to form a syrup. Stir in the blackberries, reserving a handful for the garnish, and cook for a further 5 minutes. The blackberries should still retain their shape. Remove from the heat, add the remaining blueberries, and fold through the hot mixture until they split and release their juices, but still retain their shape.

3 Fold through 1 teaspoon of the rosewater and taste. Add another teaspoon, if needed.

4 Spoon some of the juices over the bread, then fill the basin with the fruit. Make sure the fruit is packed well into the basin. Top with an even layer of bread, ensuring the fruit is completely covered.

5 If there is any juice remaining, spoon this over the top layer of bread. Stand the basin in a dish to catch any overspill of juice. Cover with cling film and place a small plate on top. Place a weight on the plate and chill overnight. Turn out onto a large plate to serve.

The rich berry syrup takes on a delicate floral note from the addition of rosewater.

PREP 15 MINUTES, PLUS CHILLING
COOK 15 MINUTES
SERVES 4

TIM ANDERSON
Champion 2011

My name is Tim Anderson and I won *MasterChef* in 2011. I have since written two cookbooks, opened my own Japanese soul food restaurant, Nanban, in London, and have appeared regularly on radio.

Q What's your favourite moment from your time on the show?

A Cooking alongside Wylie Dufresne at wd~50 in New York was an incredible experience that a lot of chefs would love to have, so I'm very grateful for that.

Q What was the first recipe you really made your own?

A It was early on in the *MasterChef* application process. You have to bring in some food that you make at home. I made a Japanese bento, but using some British ingredients, such as smoked mackerel. That was probably the first time I thought about the kind of food I wanted to do on the show.

Q What was your worst kitchen moment?

A Probably the worst day I had on *MasterChef* was when I was cooking in Australia with John Torode for his friends and family. I had to make a soufflé and an ice cream, and pretty much everything that could go wrong did go wrong. The ice cream didn't set, the soufflé exploded - it was a disaster, and I thought my *MasterChef* career was over. But John was lovely, calm and cool, and helped me fix it, and in the end it wasn't that bad.

Q What's your favourite kitchen tool and why?

A It's a bit technical and not very sexy: a probe thermometer. There's no better way to judge whether your meat, fish, even your breads are cooked. It's also good to check your food is cold enough in the fridge.

Q Who is your biggest food hero and why?

A Being a ramen chef, the people I look up to most are the ramen chefs in Japan, who are dedicated to the craft of making a perfect bowl of ramen. It's not fine dining - that's one of its joys - but a lot of work and skill goes into it.

Q Best meal of the day: breakfast, lunch, or dinner?

A I don't eat breakfast every day, but I love it, particularly fish. It's energising and satisfying without being heavy.

Q Any advice for potential MasterChefs?

A Pick a few things you want to get good at and get good at them - whether that's cooking a steak or making a bowl of noodles. Making half a dozen things that are really impressive will get you far.

PUMPKIN PIE WITH KICAP MANIS BUTTERSCOTCH SAUCE

American-style pumpkin pie is served with an unusual sauce in this recipe. Rich, sweet butterscotch is boosted with touch of thick, molasses-like kicap manis.

Kicap manis (sweet soy sauce) adds an umami note to the homemade butterscotch.

FOR THE SWEET SHORTCRUST PASTRY

150g (5½oz) plain flour, plus extra for dusting

100g (3½oz) unsalted butter, chilled and cut into cubes

50g (1¾oz) caster sugar

1 egg yolk

½ tsp vanilla extract

FOR THE FILLING

3 eggs

100g (3½oz) soft light brown sugar

1 tsp ground cinnamon

1 tsp mixed spice

200ml (7fl oz) double cream

425g can processed pumpkin, or 400g (14oz) roasted and puréed pumpkin

demerara sugar, to serve

FOR THE SAUCE

25g (scant 1oz) butter

100g (3½oz) dark soft brown sugar

2 tbsp kicap manis

1 tbsp vanilla extract

200ml (7fl oz) double cream

1 First, make the sweet shortcrust pastry (see p247). Wrap in cling film and chill for 1 hour.

2 Preheat the oven to 180°C (350°F/Gas 4). Roll out the pastry on a floured surface to a thickness of 3mm (⅛in). If it crumbles, knead it together gently. Line a 23cm (9in) loose-bottomed tart tin with the pastry, leaving an overhang of at least 2cm (¾in). Prick the base all over with a fork, then blind bake for 20 minutes (see p247). Remove the beans and paper; if the centre looks damp or raw, return it to the oven for 5 minutes.

3 Meanwhile, make the filling. In a large bowl, whisk the eggs, sugar, spices, and cream together until well blended, then beat in the pumpkin until smooth.

4 Partially pull out an oven rack from the centre of the oven. Set the pastry case (still in its tin) on the rack. Pour the filling into the case and slide the rack back into the oven. Bake for 45–50 minutes until set, and bubbles begin to form around the edge. Trim the pastry edge with a sharp knife while still warm, then leave the pie to cool completely.

5 For the sauce, melt the butter and sugar together in a pan, then whisk in the remaining ingredients. Bring to the boil, then remove from the heat and leave to cool slightly.

6 Remove the pie from the tin, divide into slices, and transfer to plates. Dust the top of each slice with a layer of demerara sugar and use a blowtorch to caramelize it.

PREP 35 MINUTES, PLUS CHILLING
COOK 1 HOUR 25 MINUTES, PLUS COOLING
SERVES 8

BOOZY MANHATTAN CHILLED CHEESECAKE

This classic no-cook cheesecake is brought bang up to date with a salty-sweet base, a tangy filling, and a Manhattan cocktail-flavoured topping from soaking cherries in a mixture of bourbon and vermouth.

MAKE IT
extraordinary

Soak cherries in bourbon and vermouth for an authentic Manhattan-flavoured topping.

75g (2½oz) unsalted butter

100g (3½oz) digestive biscuits, crushed

100g (3½oz) salted biscuits, such as Ritz crackers or pretzels, crushed

2 x 250g tubs of full-fat cream cheese

75g (2½oz) golden caster sugar

grated zest and juice of 4 lemons

140ml (4½fl oz) double cream

1 gelatine leaf, cut into small pieces

350g (12oz) fresh cherries, pitted

150ml (5fl oz) bourbon

50ml (2fl oz) red vermouth

1 strip orange peel

2 tbsp sugar

2 tbsp redcurrant jelly

1 Grease and line the cake tin. Melt the butter in a pan, add the crushed biscuits and crackers or pretzels, and stir until thoroughly coated. Transfer the mixture to the tin, pressing it down firmly with the back of a spoon.

2 Mix together the cream cheese, caster sugar, and zest. In a separate bowl, whisk the cream with an electric hand whisk until it forms soft peaks. Add the cheese mixture to the whipped cream and beat with a wooden spoon to combine.

3 In a small pan, soak the gelatine in the lemon juice for 5 minutes to soften. Then gently heat, but do not boil, stirring to dissolve. Leave to cool slightly. Add to the cheese mixture and stir well. Then pour the mixture on top of the biscuit base, spreading it out evenly. Place in the fridge for at least 2 hours, or until set and firm.

4 Place the cherries in a pan with the bourbon, vermouth, orange peel, and sugar, and stir over a high heat for 2–3 minutes, until the juices run. Carefully lift out the cherries with a slotted spoon. Stir the redcurrant jelly into the liquid until dissolved. Bring to the boil, then simmer until reduced by about three-quarters. Leave to cool.

5 To serve, transfer the cheesecake to a serving plate, arrange the cherries on top, and spoon over the sauce.

PREP 35 MINUTES, PLUS CHILLING
COOK 20 MINUTES
SERVES 6

BANANA EGGY BREAD WITH SALTED CARAMEL AND VANILLA CREAM

Whether you prefer to call it eggy bread or French toast, this recipe turns thick slices of classic banana bread into a sweet brunch or indulgent, caramel-drizzled dessert.

MAKE IT
extraordinary

Banana bread is already a treat – this recipe takes it to another level.

Pecans give the banana bread added crunch and pair perfectly with the salted caramel sauce.

FOR THE BANANA BREAD

175g (6oz) sugar

125g (4½oz) butter, plus extra for greasing

3 tbsp milk

2 eggs

1 tbsp honey

3 bananas, mashed to a smooth purée

1 tsp vanilla paste

½ tsp ground cinnamon

½ tsp grated nutmeg

250g (9oz) self-raising flour

pinch of salt

50g (1¾oz) pecan nuts, roughly chopped

FOR THE SALTED CARAMEL

250g caster sugar

50g butter

150ml (5fl oz) double cream

1 tsp salt

FOR THE VANILLA CREAM

300ml (10fl oz) double cream

3 tbsp icing sugar, plus extra for dusting

1 tbsp vanilla paste

FOR THE EGG MIX

2 eggs

3 tbsp milk

cooking spray

1 Preheat the oven to 180°C (350°F/Gas 4). In a bowl, cream the sugar and butter until pale and fluffy. Pour in the milk, then add the eggs one at a time, whisking continuously. Add the honey, banana purée, vanilla, and spices. Whisk until smooth. Sift in the flour and salt, and fold in to incorporate. Fold in the pecans.

2 Line a 450g (1lb) bread tin with baking parchment and grease with a little butter. Pour in the cake mixture, and bake for 1 hour, or until a skewer comes out clean. Leave to cool to room temperature. Cut into slices 1.5cm (½in) thick.

3 Meanwhile, make the salted caramel. Put the sugar, butter, and 5 tbsp water into a non-stick frying pan and place over a medium heat until dissolved. Do not stir. Once the mixture is golden brown and has begun to smell like caramel, give the pan a swirl, and remove from the heat. Add the double cream and salt, and whisk until smooth. Set aside.

4 For the vanilla whipped cream, place all the ingredients in a bowl and whisk until thickened to medium peaks. Set aside until ready to serve.

5 Whisk the eggs and milk in a bowl until well combined. Dip the slices of banana bread in the bowl and turn a few times to soak up the eggy mixture. Heat a frying pan over a medium heat and add a few squirts of the cooking spray. Shake the slices to remove any excess mixture, then fry for 2 minutes on each side, until golden brown. Drain on kitchen paper. Serve with a dusting of icing sugar, a dollop of whipped cream, and a generous drizzle of salted caramel.

PREP 25 MINUTES
COOK 1 HOUR 15 MINUTES
SERVES 4

CHERRY AND HAZELNUT CHOCOLATE ROULADE

This flavour-packed take on a Swiss roll brings together chocolate, cherries, and hazelnut, with maraschino and Frangelico liqueurs adding a note of sophistication.

3 eggs

85g (3oz) caster sugar

85g (3oz) plain flour

3 tbsp cocoa powder

½ tsp baking powder

3 tbsp hazelnut liqueur, such as Frangelico

3 tbsp maraschino cherries

icing sugar, for dusting

FOR THE HAZELNUT BRITTLE

110g (4oz) caster sugar

20g lightly toasted hazelnuts roughly chopped

FOR THE ICING

200ml (7fl oz) double cream

140g (5oz) dark chocolate, chopped

5–6 tsp maraschino liqueur, or syrup from the cherries

1 Make the brittle. Line a baking sheet with baking parchment. Heat the sugar with 55ml (2fl oz) water in a heavy-based pan over a medium heat, without stirring, for about 10 minutes, until golden. Add the nuts and quickly pour onto the baking sheet. Allow to cool and harden, then break into pieces and set aside.

2 Preheat the oven to 180°C (350°F/Gas 4). In a large bowl, whisk the eggs with the sugar and 1 tbsp water for about 5 minutes, until pale and light, and the whisk leaves a trail. Sift the flour, cocoa, and baking powder over the beaten eggs, and fold in. Pour the mixture into a lined Swiss roll tin, and bake for 12 minutes, until the top is springy. Remove from the oven. While still warm, brush the sponge with the hazelnut liqueur until it is all absorbed, then turn it out onto a new piece of greaseproof paper. Peel off the paper from the base of the sponge and discard. Roll up the sponge, leaving the new paper inside, then set aside to cool.

3 Make the icing. Pour the cream into a small pan, bring to the boil, then remove from the heat. Add the chocolate and the maraschino liqueur or cherry syrup and leave to melt, stirring occasionally. Allow to cool and thicken.

4 Carefully unroll the sponge, discarding the paper. Spread one-third of the icing over the sponge, scatter with half the cherries, then roll it up again. Place on a board, seam-side down. Spread the remaining icing over the top, sides, and ends of the cake. Smooth the icing with a warm palette knife, then arrange the remaining cherries and shards of hazelnut brittle along the top. Transfer to a serving board and scatter around the remaining pieces of brittle to serve.

MAKE IT *extraordinary*

Hazelnut liqueur in the sponge echoes the flavour of the nutty brittle topping.

Use the marachino cherries' rich syrup to flavour the glossy dark chocolate icing.

PREP 30 MINUTES, PLUS COOLING
COOK 30 MINUTES
SERVES 6

RASPBERRY LEMON ITALIAN MERINGUE PIE

With a layer of tart raspberry jam beneath the lemon curd, and neatly piped mounds of Italian meringue on top, this is a restaurant-standard take on a classic dessert.

45g (1½oz) butter, cut into cubes, plus extra for greasing

1 tbsp freeze-dried raspberries, plus extra to decorate

6 egg yolks, at room temperature

3 tbsp plain flour, plus extra for dusting

3 tbsp cornflour

450g (1lb) caster sugar

juice of 3 lemons

1 tbsp finely grated lemon zest

150g (5½oz) smooth raspberry jam

4 egg whites, at room temperature

micro lemon verbena, to decorate (optional)

FOR THE SWEET SHORTCRUST PASTRY

100g (3½oz) unsalted butter, chilled and cut into cubes

150g (5½oz) plain flour, plus extra for dusting

50g (1¾oz) caster sugar

1 egg yolk

½ tsp vanilla extract

1 Preheat the oven to 200°C (400°F/Gas 6). Lightly grease a 23cm (9in) loose-bottomed tart tin. Prepare the pastry (see p247), roll it out on a floured surface and use it to line the tin. Gently press the freeze-dried raspberries into the pastry. Place on a baking tray and blind bake (see p247) for 10–15 minutes, or until pale golden. Remove the paper and beans and bake for 5 minutes until golden, then remove from the oven to cool. Reduce the oven temperature to 180°C (350°F/Gas 4).

2 Lightly beat the 6 egg yolks in a bowl. Combine the flour, cornflour, and 225g (8oz) of sugar in a saucepan. Slowly add 360ml (12fl oz) of water and heat gently, stirring until the sugar dissolves. Increase the heat slightly and stir for 3–5 minutes, or until it starts to thicken. Beat several spoonfuls of the hot mixture into the egg yolks. Pour this back into the pan and slowly bring to the boil, stirring. Boil for 3 minutes, then stir in the lemon juice, zest, and butter. Boil for another 2 minutes or until thick and glossy, stirring constantly. Remove from the heat, cover, and keep warm.

3 Place the pastry case on a baking tray. Spread an even layer of jam over the base, then pour in the lemon filling. Bake for 12–15 minutes, or until lightly golden. Transfer the tart to a wire rack to cool completely before removing it from the tin.

4 Prepare a sugar syrup using the remaining sugar and 90ml (3fl oz) water (see p248). Use this syrup and the 4 egg whites to make Italian meringue (see p249). To serve, spread an even layer of meringue on each plate, then brown with a blowtorch. Spoon the remaining meringue into a piping bag fitted with a wide round nozzle. Place a slice of tart on top of the meringue, then pipe neat mounds of meringue onto the slice. Brown the piped meringue with a blowtorch. Garnish with freeze-dried raspberries and micro lemon verbena, if using.

Freeze-dried raspberries add a pop of colour and a sharp tang to complement the lemon curd.

Micro lemon verbena has a light, aromatic taste. Use to garnish the dish if you are able to source it.

Made with a hot sugar syrup, Italian meringue does not need to be baked in an oven.

PREP 25 MINUTES, PLUS CHILLING
COOK 1 HOUR, PLUS COOLING
SERVES 12

MANGO AND LIME DRIZZLE CAKE

Not only does this drizzle cake recipe substitute tart lime juice for the usual lemon juice, but the addition of freshly cut mango in the batter makes each slice moist, sweet, and out of the ordinary.

150g (5½oz) unsalted butter, softened

150g (5½oz) unrefined golden caster sugar

3 eggs

finely grated zest of 2 limes

1 large mango, peeled and roughly cubed into 1.5cm/½in pieces (about 185g/6½oz total weight)

150g (5½oz) self-raising flour, sifted

FOR THE TOPPING

4 tbsp lime juice

75g (2½oz) unrefined golden caster sugar

1 tbsp orange blossom water (optional)

icing sugar, for dusting

dried mango pieces, for decoration

lime zest, for decoration

1 Preheat the oven to 180°C (350°F/Gas 4). In a large bowl, cream together the butter and sugar with an electric hand whisk until light and fluffy. Whisk in the eggs one at a time, then add the lime zest and whisk again to combine.

2 Fold in the flour until just incorporated and then fold in the fresh mango pieces. Pour the batter into a lined 18cm (7in) round cake tin. Bake in the centre of the oven for 30–35 minutes, until well risen and a skewer inserted into the middle of the cake comes out clean.

3 To make the topping, gently heat the lime juice and sugar in a small pan until the sugar has dissolved. Remove from heat and add the orange blossom water (if using). Prick the cake all over with a thin skewer and, leaving it in the tin, carefully pour the lime and sugar mixture all over the top, a little at a time, until absorbed.

4 Allow the topping to cool. Remove the cake from the tin, dust with icing sugar, and decorate with dried mango pieces and a scattering of lime zest before serving.

A handful of dried mango pieces makes a simple yet bold decoration for the cake.

Be sure to use a just-ripe mango: the fruit should feel slightly soft but not mushy.

Before squeezing a lime, firmly roll it back and forth over a work surface: this will release the juice.

PREP 20 MINUTES
COOK 40 MINUTES
SERVES 8

HONEY CHEESECAKE WITH MACADAMIA OAT CLUSTERS

Reimagine vanilla cheesecake as a deconstructed, brunch-ready dish with this recipe. The cheesecake "filling" is sweetened with honey, the base is turned into nutty oat clusters, and fresh strawberries are macerated with black pepper to enhance their flavour.

FOR THE CLUSTERS
265g (9½oz) butter
230g (8oz) plain flour
230g (8oz) sugar
pinch of salt
180g (6oz) oats
130g (4½oz) chopped macadamia nuts
150g (5½oz) runny honey

FOR THE CHEESECAKE
250g (9oz) cream cheese
seeds of ½ vanilla pod
150g (5½oz) honey
250ml (9fl oz) double cream

FOR THE STRAWBERRIES
400g (14oz) strawberries, hulled and quartered
1 tbsp lemon juice
1 tbsp caster sugar
2 large pinches of freshly ground black pepper

1 Preheat the oven to 200°C (400°F/Gas 6). To make the clusters, rub together the butter, flour, sugar, and salt until it resembles sand. Add the oats and macadamia nuts, then stir in the honey. Mix together until small clusters form. Spread onto a baking tray. Chill the clusters in the fridge for about 20 minutes, then bake in the oven for about 15 minutes, until golden brown. Allow to cool. If you are not using them immediately, store the baked clusters in an airtight container.

2 Beat the cream cheese, vanilla seeds, and honey in a bowl to combine. Add the cream and whip until stiff. Place the mixture into a piping bag and chill in the fridge until needed.

3 In a bowl, mix the strawberries with the lemon juice and sugar, and leave to macerate for 15–20 minutes. Add the black pepper and mix well. Leave for another 5 minutes for the flavours to develop before serving.

4 To assemble, pipe three cheesecake mounds onto each serving plate, sprinkle with the clusters, and spoon over some macerated strawberries.

MAKE IT *extraordinary*

Scrape the seeds from half a vanilla pod to give the "filling" a natural sweetness.

Macadamia nut and oat clusters offer far more crunch than a cheesecake's usual biscuit base.

While it may seem strange, black pepper draws out the sweetness of the strawberries.

PREP 30 MINUTES, PLUS CHILLING AND MACERATING
COOK 15 MINUTES
SERVES 4

ALMOND CRUMBLE MINCE PIES

Mince pies may be a Christmas staple, but that doesn't mean they can't be updated. This recipe swaps the pastry lids for a nutty crumble and crystallized orange slices.

MAKE IT
extraordinary

The crystallized orange slices echo the flavours of the liqueur and citrus zest in the filling.

1 small cooking apple, peeled and grated

30g (1oz) butter, melted

85g (3oz) sultanas

85g (3oz) raisins

55g (1¾oz) currants

45g (1½oz) mixed peel, chopped

45g (1½oz) chopped almonds or hazelnuts

finely grated zest of 1 lemon

finely grated zest of 1 mandarin

1 tsp mixed spice

pinch each of grated nutmeg and ground cinnamon

1 tbsp each of brandy and orange liqueur

50g (1¾oz) vegetarian suet

30g (1oz) muscovado or soft dark brown sugar

200g (7oz) plain flour, plus extra for dusting

1 tbsp icing sugar, plus extra for dusting

140g (5oz) unsalted butter, cold

zest of 1 lemon

1 egg yolk

50g (1¾oz) fresh cranberries

FOR THE CRUMBLE

25g (scant 1oz) each ground almonds, flaked almonds, and soft brown sugar

pinch of ground cinnamon

25g (scant 1oz) unsalted butter

FOR THE ORANGE SLICES

1-2 oranges, sliced horizontally

100g (3½oz) sugar

1 Make the orange slices a day in advance. Preheat the oven to 85°C (175°F/Gas ¼). Combine the sugar and 100ml (3½fl oz) water in a pan to make a syrup (see p248). Line a baking tray with a silicone mat. Using tongs, carefully dip the orange slices into the syrup, then lay them out on the lined tray and bake for 12-14 hours, until hard and glass-like.

2 Combine the apple, butter, dried fruit, mixed peel, nuts, zest, spices, brandy, orange liqueur, suet, and muscovado sugar in a large bowl and mix well.

3 To make the pastry, sift the flour and icing sugar onto a large sheet of greaseproof paper, then tip it into the bowl of a food processor. Cut the butter into small pieces and add to the flour, along with the zest and egg yolk. Pulse the blade until the mixture resembles fine breadcrumbs. Then, with the motor running, slowly pour in enough cold water until the pastry comes together in a ball. Wrap it in cling film and leave to rest in the fridge for 20 minutes.

4 Preheat the oven to 190°C (375°F/Gas 5). Roll out the chilled pastry on a lightly floured surface to a thickness of 2mm (⅛in), and cut out 18 circles using a large biscuit cutter. Line shallow bun pans with the pastry circles, then leave to rest in the fridge.

5 Meanwhile, make the crumble by mixing together the dry ingredients and rubbing in the butter. Remove the tins from the fridge and place 1 heaped tsp of filling in each pastry case, followed by 2-3 fresh cranberries. Sprinkle over the crumble topping. Bake for 10-12 minutes, or until the pastry is golden. Carefully remove from the tins and cool on a wire rack. Dust with icing sugar. Halve the orange slices and remove the rind using scissors. Use the slices to decorate the pies.

A crunchy, flaky almond crumble tops the sweet, sticky mince pies.

PREP 40 MINUTES, PLUS CHILLING
COOK 14 HOURS 20 MINUTES
MAKES 18

KIRSCH CHERRY CHRISTMAS PUDDING

Make this kirsch-soaked, cherry-filled Christmas pudding the centrepiece of your festive dinner table. Bake it 1–2 months in advance, then re-steam before serving.

FOR THE PUDDING

85g (3oz) raisins

60g (2oz) currants

100g (3½oz) sultanas

115g (4oz) mixed dried fruit, such as figs, dates, and cherries

45g (1½oz) mixed peel, chopped

finely grated zest and juice of 1 orange

finely grated zest and juice of 1 lemon

150ml (5fl oz) kirsch, plus extra for feeding

3 tbsp black treacle

1 large cooking apple, grated

50g (2oz) fresh white breadcrumbs

50g (2oz) plain flour

1 tbsp mixed spice

100g (3½ oz) blanched almonds, chopped

2 eggs, beaten

115g (4oz) butter, chilled, plus extra for greasing

TO SERVE

500g (1lb 2oz) kirsch-marinated cherries

2 tbsp sugar

1 Combine all the dried fruit, mixed peel, orange and lemon zest and juice, kirsch, and treacle in a large bowl. Mix well, cover, and leave to stand for at least 2 hours, preferably overnight.

2 Preheat the oven to 180°C (350°F/Gas 4). Grease a 1.8 litre (3¼ pint) pudding basin with butter and line with greaseproof paper. To the dried fruit mixture, add the apple, breadcrumbs, flour, spice, almonds, and eggs. Grate the butter into the mixture and mix well. Spoon the mixture into the basin and level the surface. Cover with 2 pleated layers of greaseproof paper, measuring about 30cm (12in) square. Tie securely under the rim with string.

3 Cover the basin with a circle of foil and press down to seal the edges. Stand it in a deep-sided, heavy roasting tin. Pour in 1.7 litres (3 pints) of boiling water. Cover the whole roasting tin with a tent of foil, carefully transfer to the oven, and cook for 6 hours. Remove the basin from the roasting tin and leave the pudding to cool, keeping it in the basin.

4 If making the pudding in advance, store the pudding in a cool, dry place for 1–2 months, feeding it every 2 weeks with 1–2 spoonfuls of kirsch. To reheat the pudding before serving, steam for 1½–2 hours using the method in Step 3.

5 To serve, hollow out the centre of the pudding. Warm the cherries in a pan with their marinade, then remove them and put in the hollowed-out pudding. Place an inverted plate over the basin and turn right-side up, removing the basin. Add the sugar to the marinade and heat until dissolved. Ladle a few spoonfuls over the pudding and serve. Alternatively, carefully set the marinade alight with a long match, then pour over the hot pudding before serving.

MAKE IT *extraordinary*

Fill the steamed kirsch pudding with kirsch-soaked cherries for a fruity surprise when serving.

Dried fruits, including figs, dates, and cherries, give the pudding plenty of flavour.

PREP 35 MINUTES, PLUS STANDING
COOK 6 HOURS 10 MINUTES
SERVES 4

SEGMENT CITRUS FRUITS

With a sharp knife, cut off the top and bottom of the fruit so it can stand upright. Holding it firmly with a fork, slice down and around the flesh, following the contour of the skin. Try to remove as much of the bitter white pith as possible.

Holding the peeled fruit steady on the board with one hand, cut along the lines of the membrane that separates each slice. Repeat slicing between each membrane to remove the neat, pith-free segments.

PREPARE CITRUS PEEL

When buying citrus fruits for the peel, try to select unwaxed fruits. Wash and dry the skin, then use a peeler to remove strips of the zest, taking off as little bitter pith as possible.

If any pith remains on the peel, use a sharp knife to slice it off by running your knife along the peel, away from you. Then slice the peel into strips according to the recipe.

SKIN AND DESEED TOMATOES

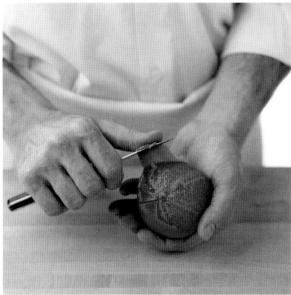

Use a sharp knife to score an "X" through the skin of the tomato at its base. Completely immerse it in boiling water for around 20 seconds, or until you can see the skin begin to split, then remove and plunge into a bowl of iced water.

When the tomato is cool enough to handle, use a paring knife to peel off the skin, starting at the base where you made the "X". Slice the tomato in half, then gently squeeze it in your hand over a bowl to force the seeds out and discard them.

PREPARE AVOCADOES

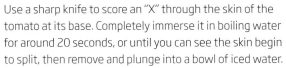

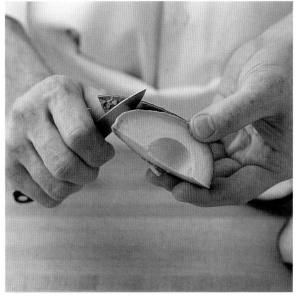

Holding the avocado firmly in one hand, cut through the skin and flesh with a chef's knife, slicing all the way around the stone. Gently twist the two halves to separate them. Strike the cutting edge of your knife into the stone to remove it.

Use a wooden spoon to prise the knife from the stone. Discard the stone. Quarter the avocado, then use a paring knife to peel away the skin from each quarter, taking care not to damage the flesh. Slice or chop as required.

PREPARE PRAWNS

To remove the intestinal vein, cut lightly along the back of the prawn with a paring knife. Remove the vein with your fingers or the knife tip, and rinse the prawn under cold running water.

To butterfly a prawn, cut along the deveined back of the prawn and splay it open, taking care not to cut all the way through. Rinse under cold running water and pat dry with kitchen paper.

CLEAN MUSSELS

As mussels are cooked and often served in their shells, they must be thoroughly cleaned. Scrub the mussels under cold running water to brush away any grit, and scrape off barnacles with a small knife.

Live mussels usually have a fibrous attachment, called a "beard", which needs to be removed. Pinch the stringy thread between your finger and thumb and firmly jerk it away from the mussel shell.

PREPARE SCALLOPS

Scrub the shell under cold running water before you open the scallop. Slide a knife between the top and bottom shell to open it, then carefully detach the scallop from the bottom shell with the knife.

Pull away and discard the viscera and frilled membrane. You can leave the cream and orange coral (roe) attached to the scallop, or remove it too if you wish. Gently rinse the scallop under cold running water.

PREPARE SWEETBREADS

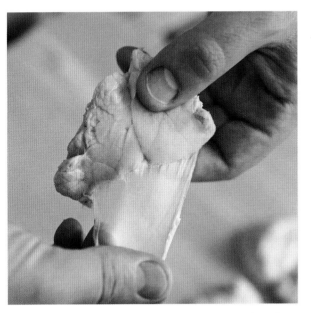

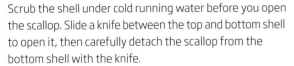

Soak the sweetbreads in cold water for 12 hours, changing the water every 3-4 hours. Peel off as much of the filament and patches of blood as possible. The filament is firm enough that it should peel off easily.

Soak the sweetbreads again, in a solution of 1 tablespoon of vinegar per 1.5 litres (2¾ pints) cold water, for a further 1-2 hours. Then peel off any remaining filament plus any small tubes that are to be found in and around the pieces.

POACH EGGS

Carefully crack an egg onto a small plate, then slide it into a pan of gently boiling water mixed with a drop of vinegar. Using a slotted spoon, gently lift the white over the yolk.

Poach in the gently boiling water for around 3–5 minutes. Before serving, place the eggs in another pan of simmering salted water for 30 seconds to remove any vinegar taste.

MAKE MAYONNAISE

Whisk together the egg yolks, mustard, and vinegar in a bowl. Pour in the oil, drop by drop, whisking all the time.

Gradually increase the speed of pouring to a steady stream. Once all the oil has been added, stir in the lemon juice.

MAKE SWEET SHORTCRUST PASTRY

Sift the plain flour onto a work surface. Make a well in the centre and add the butter, sugar, and egg yolks. Using your fingertips, work the flour into the butter and egg mixture.

When rough crumbs have formed, gather the dough into a ball and knead lightly until it is pliable. Wrap in cling film and chill for 30 minutes before using.

BLIND BAKE

Cut a circle of baking parchment slightly larger than the tart tin that you are using. Fold the disc in half several times, then clip the outer edge with scissors. Place the pastry in the tin and and prick it all over with a fork.

Cover the base and sides of the pastry with the parchment, taking the paper above the sides of the tin. Fill with baking beans and bake according to your recipe. Remove the paper and beans and return to the oven to bake again if required.

PREPARE GELATINE

Soak the required number of leaves of gelatine in enough cold water, or other liquid, to cover them fully for at least 10 minutes. Squeeze out as much of the liquid as possible before using.

In a saucepan, warm some water or whatever liquid is specified in your chosen recipe. Add the gelatine, and stir to allow it to dissolve thoroughly into the liquid, then leave to cool as instructed in the recipe.

MAKE SUGAR SYRUP

Heat your measured amount of sugar and water in a heavy-based pan over a low heat, without stirring, until dissolved. Use a wet pastry brush to wipe the pan edge to stop grains of sugar sticking.

When the sugar has dissolved, slowly heat the syrup until it reaches boiling point. Boil bring for 2 minutes to make a basic syrup, or heat to a required temperature if specified by the recipe, checking with a sugar thermometer.

MAKE MERINGUE

In a large bowl, whisk the egg whites and half the caster sugar at a moderate speed. Continue whisking until the mixture becomes smooth, shiny, and firm. Draw the whisk out of the mixture to check that soft peaks form (see p251).

Using a rubber spatula, gently fold in the rest of the sugar. Bake according to the recipe until just golden, then turn off the heat and leave the meringue to dry in the oven for the time stated in the recipe.

MAKE ITALIAN MERINGUE

Dissolve the caster sugar in water over a low heat and heat the syrup according to your recipe. Whisk the egg whites until they form soft peaks. Pour the hot sugar syrup into the egg whites, whisking continuously.

Continue to whisk until the meringue is cold, very stiff, and has a smooth and satiny consistency. Transfer into a piping or pastry bag fitted with a metal tip. To cook, brown the meringue with a blowtorch for a few minutes.

PREPARING HERBS

To chop the leaves of herbs with tender stems, such as basil, roll the leaves together into a tight bunch. Slice across the bunch with a sharp chef's knife to create fine shreds.

To strip the leaves from herbs with woody stalks, such as rosemary, run the thumb and forefinger of one hand down the stalk from top to bottom.

MAKING HERB OIL

Heat the oil specified by your recipe in a small pan to 80°C (175°F). Remove from the heat and carefully pour the oil into a blender. Add the prepared herbs and blitz until smooth.

Strain the oil through a fine sieve or muslin. If using muslin, squeeze it to extract as much oil as possible. Discard any solids and use the oil as directed in your recipe.

GLOSSARY

BASTE
To moisten food while cooking, usually with its own juices.

BEURRE NOISETTE
Butter melted and cooked until golden-brown.

BLANCH
To immerse something briefly in boiling water, then remove and plunge it into ice-cold water to prevent further cooking.

BLIND BAKE
To cook a tart or pie shell before adding its filling (see p247).

BRÛLÉE
To heat a layer of sugar until it caramelizes, usually with a blow torch or grill.

DEBEARD
To remove the fibrous attachment, known as a "beard", from a mussel (see p244).

DEGLAZE
To add liquid to a pan to dissolve any cooking residue and absorb its flavour for a gravy or sauce.

DEVEIN
To remove the intestinal vein from a prawn (see p244).

DRY FRY
To cook in a frying pan without oil or butter. Used for foods that release their own fat or oil, such as nuts or bacon.

FIRM PEAKS
The stage during whisking when firm peaks form as the whisk is lifted, and retain their shape.

FOLD
To combine a light, airy mixture with other ingredients without knocking the air out. The lighter element is added on top of the heavier one and combined gently by lifting from the bottom to the top with a spatula.

GLAZE
To coat a food with liquid or sauce to make it shiny, such as dipping meat in a sauce or brushing pastry with milk or egg before cooking.

JULIENNE
To cut into long, thin strips.

MACERATE
To soften or break up a food, often fruit, by soaking it in liquid.

MUSLIN
Finely woven cotton cloth used for straining.

PIN BONE
To remove small bones from a fish fillet using tweezers.

QUENELLE
A rounded oval of soft food (such as ice cream or mousse), moulded using two spoons.

REDUCE
To boil a sauce until some of the liquid evaporates and the flavour becomes more concentrated.

RENDER
To cook meat so that any fat melts out.

SAUTÉ
To cook small pieces of food in oil or butter over a high heat.

SEAR
To briefly brown meat, fish, or poultry over a high heat.

SCORE
To make shallow cuts with a knife point, either for decoration or to help something cook evenly.

SLURRY
A mixture of flour or cornflour and water, typically used to thicken sauces and stews.

SKIM
To remove a layer of fat or scum from the top of a liquid.

SOFT PEAKS
The stage during whisking when soft peaks form as the whisk is lifted, but quickly collapse.

SWEAT
To cook sliced or chopped food, usually vegetables, in a covered pan over a very low heat so that they soften without browning.

TOP AND TAIL
To neaten fruits and vegetables by removing the top and bottom (such as stalks and roots).

TRUSS
To tie up poultry with string to hold it in a neat shape for cooking.

INDEX

Editors Amy Slack, Kate Berens
Editorial assistant Poppy Blakiston Houston
Senior art editor Sara Robin
Designer Mandy Earey
Jacket designer Nicola Powling
Jackets co-ordinator Lucy Philpott
Pre-production producer Luca Frassinetti
Print producer Luca Bazzoli
Creative technical support Sonia Charbonnier
Managing editor Stephanie Farrow
Managing art editor Christine Keilty
Art director Maxine Pedliham
Publisher Mary-Clare Jerram

Recipe photography David Loftus
Food stylist Rukmini Iyer

First published in Great Britain in 2018 by
Dorling Kindersley Limited
80 Strand, London, WC2R 0RL

A Penguin Random House Company
10 9 8 7 6 5 4 3 2 1
001–310179–Oct/2018

Acknowledgments

Shine TV and Endemol Shine Group would like to thank:
Frances Adams, David Ambler, Katie Attwood, Alice Bernardi,
Martin Buckett, Claire Burton, Bev Comboy, Kerisa Edwards,
Jessica Hannan, Sophie Harris, Aimee Joughin, Ozen Kazim,
Angela Loftus, Lou Plank, Lyndsey Posner, Franc Roddam,
Jane Smith, John Torode, and Gregg Wallace.

Special thanks go to the MasterChef champions who
supplied recipes and interviews for this book: Tim Anderson,
Dhruv Baker, Angellica Bell, Natalie Coleman, Ping Coombes,
Jane Devonshire, Mat Follas, Saliha Mahmood Ahmed, James
Nathan, Shelina Permalloo, Simon Wood.

Dorling Kindersley would like to thank:
DK would like to thank Angela Loftus for her help and
endless patience in the making of this book, David Loftus
for his superb photography, Rukmini Iyer for her wonderful
food styling, Claire Burton for reviewing the design, Jo Harris
for supplying props, and Vanessa Bird for indexing.

About the stylist

Rukmini Iyer is a food stylist and food writer, who trained
at Tom Kitchin's Michelin-starred restaurant The Kitchin
before starting work as a food stylist. She loves working
with photographers on food shoots on everything from
magazine features to cookbooks and television commercials.
The Roasting Tin, her first book on simple weekday cooking,
is out now.